HEINEMANN

Carolyn Meggitt

Child Development
An Illustrated Guide

3rd edition with DVD

ALWAYS LEARNING

PEARSON

Published by Pearson Education Limited, Edinburgh Gate, Harlow, Essex, CM20 2JE.

www.pearsonschoolsandfecolleges.co.uk
Heinemann is a registered trademark of Pearson Education Limited

Text © Carolyn Meggitt 2012
Design and layouts by Lorraine Inglis Design
Original illustrations © Pearson Education Ltd
Cover design by Pearson Education Ltd
Cover photo/illustration © Getty Images (James Baigrie)

The right of Carolyn Meggitt to be identified as author of this work has been asserted by her
in accordance with the Copyright, Designs and Patents Act 1988.

First published 2000
Second edition 2006
Third edition 2012

16 15 14
10 9 8 7 6 5 4

British Library Cataloguing in Publication Data
A catalogue record for this book is available from the British Library

ISBN 978 0 435 07880 5

Printed in Slovakia by Neografia

Acknowledgements
The author and publisher would like to thank the following individuals and organisations for
permission to reproduce photographs:

(Key: b-bottom; c-centre; l-left; r-right; t-top)
Pearson Education Ltd: Jules Selmes 1, 7b, 8tr, 8br, 10bl, 12br, 13tr, 13bl, 13br, 14, 15b, 17, 19, 20,
20c, 20bl, 21tr, 21b, 22, 27t, 27c, 28t, 28c, 28b, 29t, 29b, 30, 32, 34, 35c, 36t, 36l, 36r, 37t, 37c, 37b,
38, 39br, 40, 40b, 43c, 44t, 44cl, 44b, 45l, 45c, 45r, 46, 47br, 49, 50t, 50b, 51t, 51b, 52, 53t, 53c,
53b, 54, 57, 58t, 58l, 58r, 59tl, 59cr, 59br, 61t, 61b, 62, 63b, 65c, 66t, 66b, 67t, 67b, 70, 71c, 75, 76t,
76l, 76r, 77tr, 77l, 77cr, 77bl, 78t, 81bc, 82, 84l, 85c, 86t, 86l, 86c, 87tl, 87tr, 87b, 88, 89br, 93, 94t,
94b, 95t, 97b, 99, 101, 102t, 102bl, 103tl, 103c, 103bl, 103br, 104t, 107bc, 109, 110t, 110bl, 111t, 111b, 116,
117, 118bl, 121b, 122tr, 123b, 124, 125, 130, 132, 133b, 134b, 135, 139b, 142c, 144, 145, 146br, 147t, 147b,
148, 149b, 150r, 153b, 154br, 155r, 156cr, 157r, 159, 161, 162, 163c, 164, 169, 171, 176t, 176c, 176b, 179,
179c, 180, 183, 183t, 184t, 184l, 189, 192, 194; **Shutterstock.com:** Alena Hovorkova 172

All other images © Pearson Education

Every effort has been made to contact copyright holders of material reproduced in this book.
Any omissions will be rectified in subsequent printings if notice is given to the publishers.
Pearson Education Limited is not responsible for the content of any external internet sites. It is
essential for tutors to preview each website before using it in class so as to ensure that the URL
is still accurate, relevant and appropriate. We suggest that tutors bookmark useful websites
and consider enabling students to access them through the school/college intranet.

Contents

Acknowledgements

I would like to thank many people for their valuable assistance in producing this book.

Thank you to the parents of all the babies, children and young people whose photographs appear here and also to the children and young people themselves, including those at Faze, Faringdon Youth Centre for their patience and co-operation.

Many thanks to all the children and parents at the Robins Group, run by the SENSS Physical Disability (PD) Early Years Service, for the photographs in the section on children with additional needs, and also to all the staff, including Jackie Timms.

Also, a big thank you to Jules Selmes for his patience and skill in taking the photographs and to Caitlin Swain, Virginia Carter and Jenny Hunt for helping the photo shoots go smoothly.

Thanks to the publishing team at Pearson Education for their efficiency and enthusiasm – Virginia Carter, Jenny Hunt and Lindsay Lewis.

Foreword

The third edition of *Child Development, an Illustrated Guide* follows in the tradition of the first and second editions in its clear presentation and attractive, reader-friendly layout. The video clips contained on the DVD are an important contribution in this.

The terminology has been updated to help readers use the new English EYFS framework. Terms such as cognitive development are also used, so that readers can make links from the EYFS to child development theory. Readers using the early childhood frameworks in Scotland, Wales and Northern Ireland will be able to make good practical use of the theories presented in the book in their updated form.

In this edition the reader is introduced to research and theory contributing to our understanding of birth to 19 years. This reflects our increasing understanding of human development.

Observation is central to the development of good practice in early childhood work. Observation informs practice, helps practitioners to get to know the child (assessment) and helps practitioners to plan next steps that are just right for that child, at the right time and in the right way for learning and development to take place. To highlight the need for observation, this edition of the book includes sections throughout called 'Observation Points'.

The theories selected and referred to in the book include recent developments in neuroscience. Concrete examples are given of all the theories, which help to bring them to life. They are presented in a clear and easy-to-understand format.

Professor Tina Bruce CBE
University of Roehampton

Introduction

The idea for the first edition of this book was conceived in response to the growth of childcare courses worldwide. Many books focused on child development, but no other educational book offered a concise pictorial guide to the general development of children from birth right through to the age of eight years. The second edition covered up to the age of sixteen. In response to the recent development of courses to include child development to the age of nineteen, this third edition has a chapter covering development between twelve and nineteen years. There are new ideas for observations and new photographs in the chapter on the theories of child development which will help readers relate theory to practice.

Children across the world seem to pass through the same sequences of development, within the same broad timetables. Although the pattern is generally the same for all children, it is important to remember that each child is unique. Nevertheless, understanding the typical pattern will help you to develop your skills both in promoting children's health and in stimulating their all-round (or holistic) development.

The different areas of development are interrelated. The ideas, language, communication, feelings, relationships and other cultural elements among which each child is brought up influence his or her development profoundly.

Children with special needs often seem to dance the developmental ladder – they move through developmental stages in unusual and very uneven ways. For example, they might sit or walk at the usual age, but not talk at the usual age.

Mary Sheridan's valuable research in the 1950s provides a useful framework for the study of child development. This book extends Sheridan's work by incorporating additional research from many other experts in the field.

Simply reading statements about what a child at a given age is expected to achieve can prove very dull. I believe that presenting this information alongside photographs of real children will bring the subject of child development alive.

Carolyn Meggitt

1 Aspects of holistic child development

It is important to keep in mind that even a tiny baby is a person. *Holistic development* sees the child in the round, as a whole person – physically, emotionally, intellectually, socially, morally, culturally and spiritually.

Learning about child development involves studying patterns of growth and development, from which guidelines for 'normal' development are drawn up.

Developmental norms are sometimes called *milestones* – they describe the recognised pattern of development that children are expected to follow. Each child will develop in a *unique* way; however, using norms helps in understanding these general patterns of development while recognising the wide variation between individuals.

Based on children and young people growing up in Western Europe, the norms described in this book show what *most* children can do at particular stages.

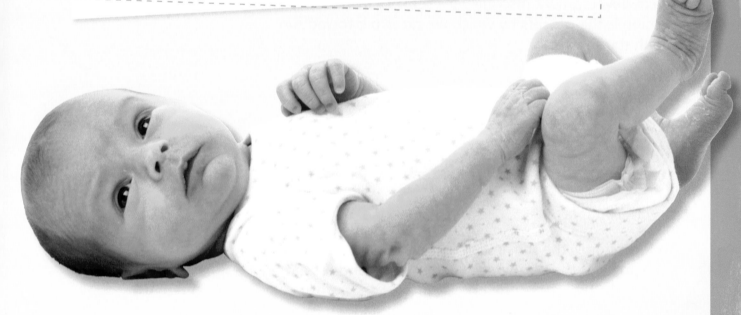

Areas of development

The areas of development described in this book are these:

Physical development

Physical development is the way in which the body increases in skill and becomes more complex in its performance. There are two main areas:

- Gross motor skills: These use the large muscles in the body, and include walking, running and climbing.
- Fine motor skills: These include gross and fine manipulative skills.
  - Gross manipulative skills involve single limb movements, usually of the arm, for example throwing, catching and making sweeping arm movements.
  - Fine manipulative skills involve precise use of the hands and fingers, for example pointing, drawing, using a knife and fork or chopsticks, writing or doing up shoelaces.

Sensory development

Physical development also includes sensory development. Sensation is the process by which we receive information through the senses:

- vision
- hearing
- smell
- touch
- taste
- proprioception.

Proprioception is the sense that tells people where the mobile parts of their body, such as the arms and legs, are in relation to the rest of the body.

Cognitive development

Cognitive or intellectual development is development of the mind – the part of the brain that is used for recognising, reasoning, knowing and understanding.

Perception involves people making sense of what they see, hear, touch, smell and taste. Perception is affected by previous experience and knowledge, and by the person's emotional state at the time.

Communication and language development

Communication is the exchange of messages or meanings. It uses all the senses, although we often focus on language and speech because they convey the most complex meanings. Language is a structured system that conveys meaning. We usually use spoken language but can also communicate using writing or sign language.

Communication and language development include the development of skills in:

- receptive speech – what a person understands
- expressive speech – the words the person produces
- articulation – the person's actual pronunciation of words.

Personal, social and emotional development

Personal development

Personal development focuses on children's acquisition of knowledge, relationship skills, thinking skills and personal capabilities. It also includes the development of emotional awareness, values and life skills.

Social development

Social development includes the growth of the child's relationships with other people. Socialisation is the process of learning the skills and attitudes that enable the child to live easily with other members of the community.

Emotional development

Emotional development is about feelings and how we deal with them:

- the growth of feelings about, and awareness of, *oneself*
- the growth of feelings towards *other people*
- the development of self-esteem and a self-concept.

Moral and spiritual development

Moral and spiritual development consists of a maturing awareness of how to relate to others ethically, morally and humanely. It involves understanding values such as honesty and respect, and acquiring concepts such as right and wrong and taking responsibility for the consequences of one's actions.

The pattern of development

Children's development follows a pattern:

From simple to complex

Development progresses from simple actions to more complex ones. For example, children stand before they can walk, and walk before they can skip or hop.

From head to toe

Development progresses downwards. Physical control and co-ordination begins with a child's head and develops down the body through the arms, hands and back, and finally to the legs and feet.

From inner to outer

Development progresses from actions nearer the body to more complex ones further from the body. For example, children can co-ordinate their arms, using gross motor skills to reach for an object, before they have learned the fine motor skills necessary to use their fingers to pick it up.

Note that during puberty there is another growth spurt; this time the growth starts at the outside of the body and works *inwards*. Hands and feet expand first; the shin bones lengthen before the thigh, and the forearm before the upper arm; finally, the spine grows.

From general to specific

Development progresses from general responses to specific ones. For example, a young baby shows pleasure by a massive general response – the eyes widen, and the legs and arms move vigorously – whereas an older child shows pleasure by smiling or using appropriate words or gestures.

The various aspects of development are intricately linked: each affects and is affected by the others. For example, once children have reached the stage of emotional development at which they feel secure when apart from their main carer, they will have access to a much wider range of relationships, experiences and opportunities for learning. Similarly, when children can use communication and language skills effectively, they will have more opportunities for social interaction. If one aspect is hampered or neglected in some way, children will be challenged in reaching their full potential.

The importance of play

Play is vital to children's all-round development. Play provides opportunities for children to:

- develop confidence, self-esteem and a sense of security
- realise their potential and feel competent
- use creativity and imagination
- develop reading, thinking and problem-solving skills as well as motor skills
- learn how to control their emotions, and understand and interpret the world around them
- learn relationship and social skills, and develop values and ethics.

ICT and child development

ICT resources for young children have two distinct features; they can communicate information and/or promote interactivity.

Communicating information	Promoting interactivity
Cameras: still and video cameras	Computers
Audiocassettes	Musical keyboards
Television, video, DVD	Activity centres
Internet	Digital interactive TV
Mobile phones	Children's websites
Email	Remote controlled toys

The introduction of ICT in nursery settings is controversial, with both televisions and computers increasingly being used as educational tools. Some educationalists think that the best thing a very young child can do with a computer or television is to play with the box it came in. By using the box as a boat, house, car or other symbol, the child is using imagination and both initiates and remains in control of the play. Others believe that carefully selected television programmes and computer software offer children of all ages a rich learning experience, which prepares them for further use of technology.

2 At birth

Newborn babies are already actively using all their senses to explore their new environment. They are seeing new things, listening to new sounds and smelling new odours. When not asleep, babies are alert. Already they are learning to cope with a huge amount of new information. Newborn babies can focus on objects less than one metre away. They show a marked preference for human faces.

They can recognise their mother's voice, and are settling into the world of noise, light, smell, taste and touch outside the womb.

Physical development

Gross motor skills

At birth, babies:

- lie supine (on their backs), with the head to one side.

Other physical positions are also characteristic:

- When placed on their front (the prone position), babies lie with the head turned to one side, the buttocks humped up and the knees tucked under the abdomen.
- When held up by a hand under the chest (ventral suspension), the head drops below the plane of the body and the arms and legs are partly bent (flexion).

▲ When pulled into a sitting position the head lags

Fine motor skills

At birth, babies:

- usually hold their hands tightly closed, but the hands may open spontaneously during feeding or when the back of the hand is stroked
- often hold their thumbs tucked in under their fingers.

▲ Ventral suspension

Sensory development

Newborn babies are already actively using all their senses to explore their new environment. These senses are sight (vision), hearing, smell, taste and touch.

Vision

Newborn babies automatically blink in response to light, sound or touch. During the first two weeks, if the baby's head turns to one side there is often a delay when the eyes remain fixed before following the head's movement. This is called the doll's eye response. Newborn babies are very near-sighted at first: they can focus best on things that are within 25 cm (10 inches) of their faces. This means that they can see well enough to focus on their parent's face when being held in their arms. Their vision is quite blurry outside this range, but they can follow a light with their eyes and turn toward lights. Sometimes babies appear to have a wandering eye or even a squint as their eyes may move independently of each other. This is normal during the early weeks of life and is because they are still gaining control of the eye muscles.

At birth, babies:

- will turn their head towards the light and will stare at bright, shiny objects
- are fascinated by human faces and gaze attentively at their carer's face when being fed or cuddled
- open their eyes when held upright
- close their eyes tightly if a pencil light is shone directly into them
- like looking at high-contrast patterns and shapes
- blink in response to sound or movement
- prefer to look at patterns – such as stripes or circles – rather than plain surfaces.
- prefer to look at things that are moving – they will focus on and follow a moving ball with their eyes, a skill known as tracking.

See clip 1 on DVD

Hearing

Babies develop a very acute sense of hearing while in the womb. Ultrasound studies have shown that unborn babies as early as 25 weeks gestation can startle in response to a sudden loud noise. Newborn babies can distinguish different voices and other sounds and they can also determine from which direction a sound is coming. For example, if a small bell is rung above a newborn baby's head, he will turn his head in the direction of the sound and watch the object making the sound. A baby often stops crying and listens to a human voice by two weeks of age.

At birth, babies:

- recognise their mother's or main carer's voice at less than one week old – and are comforted by their voice

- prefer to listen to soft, melodic speech: they can tell the difference between a calm, happy tone and an angry voice and will respond with pleasure to a soft, lilting voice and may cry when they hear a loud, angry voice

- cannot hear very soft sounds

- are startled by loud, sudden noises – such as a door banging.

◀ Baby comforted by mother's voice

Touch

Newborn babies are very sensitive to touch – particularly their faces, abdomens, hands and the soles of their feet. From the beginning, babies can feel pain. Through their senses, they also perceive the movements that they themselves make and the way that other people move them about.

At birth, babies:

- prefer to be held close, comforted, cuddled, stroked and rocked
- enjoy stroking of their skin: this action helps newborn babies to sleep, and it helps to encourage closeness between baby and parent
- like the feel of soft fabrics
- enjoy skin-to-skin contact with their parents, and being cuddled.

Taste

Newborn babies also have a well-developed sense of taste; they are born with a full set of taste-buds, although these will take time to mature.

At birth, babies:

- generally enjoy sweetness and dislike sour liquids: they can detect differences in the taste of their mother's milk, which can change depending on what the mother eats
- show that they find tastes unpleasant by screwing up their faces and trying to reject the taste from their mouth.

Smell

Newborn babies are sensitive to the smell of their mother and studies have shown that at just three days they can tell the difference between their own mother's and another mother's milk.

At birth, babies:

- are attracted not just to the smell of milk, but also to their mother's own unique body scent

- if breastfed, can distinguish the smell of their mother's breasts from those of other women who are breastfeeding

- will also turn towards pleasant smells – such as banana or vanilla – and turn away from a smell they find unpleasant – such as ammonia.

Reflexes of a newborn baby

Newborn babies display a number of reflex actions. A reflex action is one made automatically, without needing a conscious message from the brain – such as swallowing, sneezing or blinking. The presence of some of the newborn's primitive reflexes is essential to survival. The most important of these reflexes is breathing, closely followed by the rooting and sucking reflexes that help them to search out the breast and to feed successfully. Some of the reflexes are replaced by voluntary responses as the brain takes control of behaviour; for example, the grasp reflex has to fade before the baby learns to hold – and let go of – objects that are placed in her hand. Doctors check for some of these reflexes during the baby's first examination. If the reflexes persist beyond an expected time it may indicate a delay in development.

The swallowing and sucking reflexes

When anything is put in the mouth, babies at once suck and swallow. Some babies while still in the womb make their fingers sore by sucking them.

The rooting reflex

If one side of the baby's cheek or mouth is gently touched, the baby's head turns towards the touch and the mouth purses as if in search of the nipple – usually looking for food. This is very useful when learning to breastfeed a baby as it helps the baby to latch on well to the breast in the first weeks of life. This reflex should have disappeared by 3–4 months of age.

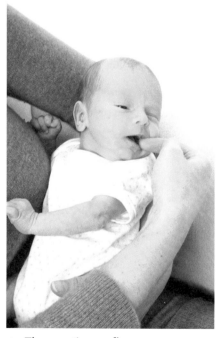

▲ The rooting reflex

The grasp reflex

This is demonstrated by placing your finger or an object into the baby's open palm, which will cause a reflex or automatic grasp or grip. If you try to pull away, the grasp will get even stronger. This reflex should have disappeared by around 3 months of age.

The stepping or walking reflex

When held upright and tilting slightly forward with their feet placed on a firm surface, babies will make forward stepping movements. This reflex is present at birth, disappears at around 2–3 months and then reappears when the child is ready to learn to walk later on.

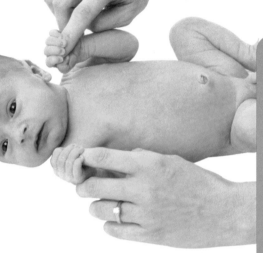

▲ The grasp reflex

The asymmetric tonic neck reflex (ATNR)

This reflex involves a coordinated movement of the baby's neck, arm and leg in conjunction with the head. If the baby's head is turned to one side, the baby will straighten the arm and leg on that side and bend the arm and leg on the opposite side. The ATNR begins about 18 weeks after conception and should be fully developed at birth. Later this reflex plays an important role in hand-eye co-ordination and object and distance perception.

▲ The asymmetric tonic neck reflex

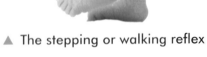

▲ The stepping or walking reflex

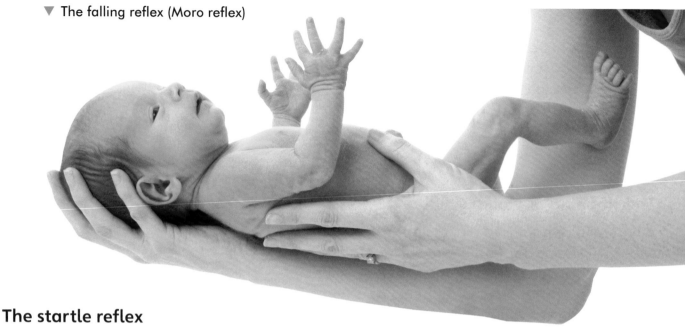

▼ The falling reflex (Moro reflex)

The startle reflex

When babies are startled by a sudden loud noise or bright light, they will move their arms outwards with elbows bent and hands clenched.

The falling reflex (Moro reflex)

This is often called the Moro reflex. Any sudden movement that affects the neck gives babies the feeling that they may be dropped; they will fling out the arms and open the hands, before bringing them back over the chest as if to catch hold of something. This reflex will disappear by 4–6 months.

Cognitive development

At birth, babies:

- are beginning to develop concepts: concepts are abstract ideas, based on the senses and combined with growing understanding (for example, babies become aware of physical sensations, such as hunger, and respond by crying)

- explore using their senses and using their own activity and movement.

Communication and language development

At birth, babies:

- need to share language experiences and co-operate with others
- make eye contact and cry to indicate need
- respond to high-pitched tones by moving their limbs
- often synchronise actions with the sound of an adult voice
- are often able to imitate, for example copying adults who open their mouth wide or stick out their tongue
- quieten when picked up
- may move their eyes towards the direction of sound.

▼ Mother and baby gazing at each other

Personal, social and emotional development

At birth, babies:

- use total body movements to express pleasure at bath time or when being fed
- enjoy feeding and cuddling
- often imitate facial expressions
- first smile in definite response to carer at around 5–6 weeks.

Play

Newborn babies respond to things that they see, hear and feel. Play might include the following:

Pullingf aces

Try sticking out your tongue and opening your mouth wide – the baby may copy you.

Showingo bjects

Try showing the baby brightly coloured woolly pompoms, balloons, shiny objects and black and white patterns. Hold the object directly in front of the baby's face, and give the baby time to focus on it. Then slowly move it.

Takingturns

Talk with babies. If you talk to babies and leave time for a response, you will find that very young babies react, first with a concentrated expression and later with smiles and excited leg kicking.

Promoting development

- Provide plenty of physical contact, and maintain eye contact.

- Massage their body and limbs during or after bathing.

- Talk lovingly to babies and give them the opportunity to respond. Hearing is an important part of language development, so it is essential that babies are talked to. Parents and other adults automatically alter the pitch of their voices when talking to babies and use a lot of repetition.

- Encourage bonding with the baby's main carers by allowing time for them to enjoy the relationship.

- Expect no set routine within the first few weeks.

- Use bright, contrasting colours in furnishings.

- Feed babies on demand, and talk and sing to them.

- Introduce them to different household noises.

- Provide contact with other adults and children.

- Encourage babies to lie on the floor and kick and experiment safely with movement.

- Provide opportunities for babies to feel the freedom of moving without a nappy or clothes on.

- Provide a mobile over the cot and/or the nappy-changing area.

- Encourage focusing and co-ordination by stringing light rattles and toys over the pram or cot.

- Recordings of 'womb music' often help to calm a newborn baby as they reproduce the rhythmic heartbeat sounds heard by the baby when in the womb.

Safety points

When playing with babies, always support the head – babies' neck muscles are not yet strong enough to control movement.

- Never leave babies with a feeding bottle propped in their mouth.
- Always place babies on their back to sleep.
- Keep the temperature in a baby's room at around 20°C (68°F).

Note to parents: The safest place for your baby to sleep is in a cot in your room for the first six months.

◄ Baby lying supine experimenting with movement

Activities

Design a mobile

Research shows that babies prefer contrasting or primary colours (not pastel shades): our brains are programmed to respond to contrasts.

1 Think of two or more designs for the mobile. (You could use a coat hanger or a cardboard tube as your basic structure.)

2 Compare your ideas, considering the following factors:

- availability of resources and materials
- skills and time required
- costs of materials
- appropriateness of the design for its purpose
- safety.

3 Based on your considerations, select one of the designs and make the mobile.

Contrastc ards

To encourage visual development, make some cards with different black and white patterns.

Attach the cards securely to the inside of the baby's pram or cot.

 Observation point

You could use this activity in preparation for a child observation.

- First, write down your instructions for making the mobile.
- Now evaluate them: were they easy to follow, or did you have to modify the original plan?
- Next, observe a baby reacting to the mobile, and record a detailed observation.
- Did the baby react as you would expect for a baby of this age and stage of development?

3 One month

By one month, babies are beginning to smile in response to adult smiles. Their cries become more expressive, and they make non-crying noises such as cooing and gurgling.

Babies enjoy kicking their legs and waving their arms about.

They may imitate facial expressions, and are able to follow moving objects with their eyes.

Physical development

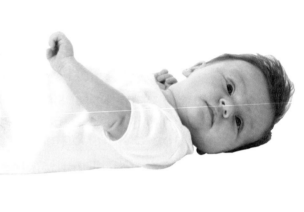

Gross motor skills

By one month, babies:

- keep their head to one side when lying on their back (supine), with the arm and the leg on the face side outstretched, the knees apart, and the soles of the feet turned inwards
- can turn from their side to their back
- will lift their head briefly from the prone position
- when held in ventral suspension, will keep the head in line with the body and the hips semi-extended
- make jerky and uncontrolled arm and leg movements
- if pulled to a sitting position, will show head lag
- are beginning to take their fists to their mouth
- open their hands from time to time.

▲ Ventral suspension: Head in line with the body and hips are semi-extended

▲ Grasping an adult's finger

Fine motor skills

By one month, babies:

- show interest and excitement by their facial expressions
- open their hands to grasp an adult's finger.

Sensory development

By one month, babies:

- focus their gaze at 20–25 cm (8–10 inches)
- turn their head towards a diffuse light source, and stare at bright, shiny objects
- may move their head towards the source of a sound, but are not yet able to locate the source
- are startled by sudden noises – when hearing a particular sound, they may momentarily 'freeze'
- blink defensively when something comes towards them
- follow the movement of a bright, dangling object moved slowly in their line of vision – this is known as tracking.

▲ Turning head towards a light source

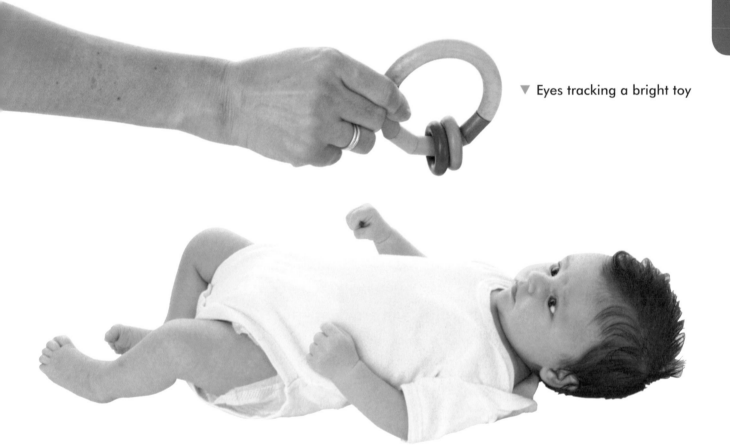

▼ Eyes tracking a bright toy

Cognitive development

By one month, babies:

- recognise their primary carers and show this by responding to them with a combination of excited movements, coos and smiles
- begin to repeat enjoyable movements, such as thumb-sucking.

Communication and language development

By one month, babies:

- make non-crying noises, such as cooing and gurgling
- cry in more expressive ways
- interact with an adult holding them up face-to-face, by simultaneously looking, listening, vocalising, and moving their arms and legs excitedly.

See clip 2 on DVD

Personal, social and emotional development

By one month, babies:

- smile in response to an adult
- gaze attentively at the adult's face when being fed
- are beginning to show a particular temperament – for example, placid or excitable
- enjoy sucking
- turn to regard a nearby speaker's face.

▶ Enjoys sucking

Play

By one month, babies:

- love to watch movement, such as trees in the wind, or moving bright, contrasting objects placed within their field of vision

- enjoy listening to the sound of bells, music and voices, and to rhythmic sounds.

Promoting development

- Use a special supporting infant chair so that babies can see adult activity.

- Let them kick freely without a nappy on.

- Gently massage the baby's body and limbs during or after bathing.

- Use brightly coloured mobiles and wind chimes over the baby's cot and/or changing mat.

- Encourage focusing and co-ordination by hanging light rattles and toys over the pram or cot.

- Talk to and smile with the baby.

- Sing while feeding or bathing the baby. Allow time for the baby to respond.

- Learn to differentiate between the baby's cries, and to respond to them appropriately.

- Encourage laughter by tickling the baby.

- Hold the baby close to promote a feeling of security.

- Try tying a few small bells safely around the baby's wrists. This encourages babies to watch their hands.

Safety points

- Never leave rattles or similar toys in a baby's cot or pram. They could become wedged in the baby's mouth and might cause suffocation.

- Do not leave a baby unattended on a table, work surface, bed or sofa. Lie the baby on the floor instead.

Activities

Followingm ovement

At around 6–10 weeks, babies begin to follow movement with their eyes. One way of promoting visual development – and of improving head–eye co-ordination – in young babies is to let them watch a moving toy.

1 Select a favourite toy – perhaps a teddy or a brightly coloured toy.

2 Hold the toy about I metre (3 feet) in front of the baby.

3 Slowly move the toy from side to side so that the baby's eyes can follow it.

4 As the baby gets better at following the movement, swing the toy further each way.

5 Try different directions – up and down, towards and away from the baby.

Babym assage

Massage has many benefits for a baby. It is very soothing and can calm a fretful baby. It is also a very good way of showing love. Parental permission should always be obtained before undertaking baby massage. The main points to remember are that the experience should:

● benefit both the baby and the carer, creating a feeling of calm and increasing the carer's confidence in handling techniques

● be conducted in a relaxed atmosphere, avoiding distractions, such as the telephone or other people

● be carried out using very gentle strokes

Observation point

Arrange for a partner to perform the activity and record an observation of the baby's reactions. Guidance will be given by your tutors regarding the format and content of any observations and you must always obtain permission from parents or tutors and observe the rules of confidentiality.

- always be symmetrical – both sides of the baby's body should be massaged at the same time
- take place in a warm room
- be an unhurried, relaxing experience.

The following is an appropriate massage sequence.

1 Prepare the room by making sure that there are no draughts and that the room is warm. Remove any jewellery and make sure that your nails have no rough edges.

2 You could use a mat with a thick towel on the floor, or simply lie the baby along your lap – make sure your own back is supported.

3 Use a baby oil. Warm it by first rubbing it between your palms.

4 Work down from the baby's head, using a light, circular motion. First massage the crown of the baby's head very gently; then move on to the forehead, cheeks and ears.

5 Gently massage the baby's neck, from the ears down to the shoulders, and from the chin to the chest.

6 Gently stroke the baby's arms, starting from the shoulders and going all the way to the fingertips.

7 Stroke down the baby's chest and tummy, rubbing in a circular direction.

8 Gently massage the baby's legs, from the thighs to the ankles.

9 Massage the baby's feet, stroking from heel to toe. Concentrate on each toe individually.

10 Finally, turn the baby over onto their front and gently massage the back.

Throughout the procedure, talk softly to the baby and always leave one hand in contact with the baby's body, to provide security and comfort. Always ensure you obtain a parent's permission before undertaking baby massage.

See also Baby Massage for the VTCT Certificate, Nyssen, C. (2003) Heinemann 978-0435456481.

 Observation point

This could also be used as an opportunity to observe the interaction between a baby and an adult. Record your observations using a variety of methods — for example narrative method illustrated by photographs.

4 Three months

By 3 months, babies are showing more interest in playthings.

They like to kick vigorously and to clasp their hands together.

They respond to familiar situations with a combination of excited movements, smiles and a variety of vocalisations, such as cries, cooing sounds and chuckles.

Physical development

Gross motor skills

At about 3 months, babies:

- keep their head in a central position when lying supine
- can now lift both their head and their chest in the prone position, supported on their forearms

▲ Lifting head and chest in prone position

- when held in ventral suspension, keep their head above the line of the body
- have almost no head lag in moving into the sitting position

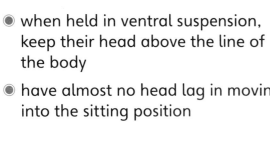

▲ Raised head in ventral suspension

◄ Almost no head lag when pulled to sitting position

◀ Straight back when sitting

- when held, can sit with their back straight
- kick vigorously, with their legs alternating or occasionally together
- can wave their arms and bring their hands together over their body.

Fine motor skills

At about 3 months, babies:
- move their head to follow adults' movements
- watch their hands and play with their fingers
- clasp and unclasp their hands at the midline of the body, and take them to the mouth
- can hold a rattle for a brief time before dropping it.

▶ Taking the hand to the mouth

◀ Eyes following a moving toy

Sensoryd evelopment

At about 3 months, babies:

- are able to focus their eyes on the same point
- can move their head deliberately to gaze around them
- prefer moving objects to still ones
- their eyes will follow a moving toy from side to side (through 180°)
- turn their eyes towards a sound source, especially a human voice
- respond to their name being called
- often suck their lips in response to the sounds of food preparation
- are distressed by sudden loud noises
- are fascinated by human faces and can recognise their mother's or main carer's face in a photograph.

Cognitive development

At about 3 months, babies:

- take an increasing interest in their surroundings
- show an increasing interest in playthings
- understand cause and effect – for example, they will deliberately shake a rattle, knowing that it will make a noise.

Communication and language development

At about 3 months, babies:

- laugh and vocalise, with increasing tone and intensity
- are becoming conversational by cooing, gurgling and chuckling – they can exchange coos with a familiar person
- smile in response to speech
- cry loudly when expressing a need.

Personal, social and emotional development

At about 3 months, babies:

- show enjoyment at caring routines, such as bathtime
- fix their eyes unblinkingly on the carer's face when feeding
- respond with obvious pleasure to loving attention and cuddles
- stay awake for longer periods of time (70 per cent of babies at this age sleep through the night)
- smile at familiar people and at strangers.

Play

At about 3 months, babies:

- enjoy holding rattles, chiming balls and musical toys
- love to explore different textures, for example on an activity mat.

Promoting development

- Use a supporting infant chair so that the baby can watch adult activity.
- Provide brightly coloured mobiles and wind chimes to encourage focusing at 20 cm (8 inches).
- Place some toys on a blanket or play mat on the floor. Let the baby lie on her or his tummy to play with the toys for short periods.
- Give the baby a rattle to hold.
- Attach objects above the cot that make a noise when touched.
- Imitate the sounds made by the baby and encourage repetition.
- Sing nursery rhymes.
- Change the baby's position frequently so that there are different things to look at and to experience.
- Encourage contact with other adults and children.
- Try action rhymes with the baby on your lap, such as *This little piggy went to market*.
- Respond to the baby's needs and show enjoyment in providing care.
- Tickle the baby to provide enjoyment.
- Massage or stroke the baby's limbs when bathing or if using massage oil.

▲ Responding with pleasure to being cuddled

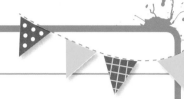

Activities

A simple game or toy

Design and make a simple game or toy that will encourage a baby's sensory development.

1 Think about the stage of development the child has reached. Plan to make a game or toy that will promote development of one or more of the baby's senses – examples are an activity mat, sound lotto, a 'feely' bag or a game of matching smells.

2 Points to consider are:

- safety
- hygiene
- suitability for the purpose.

Safety points

- Always protect babies, of all skin tones, from exposure to sunlight. Use a special sun-protection cream, a sun hat to protect the face and neck, and a pram canopy.
- Never leave small objects within reach – everything finds its way to a baby's mouth.
- When you buy goods, always check for an appropriate safety symbol.

Observation point

You could use this activity for a child observation.
- First, say which sense you hope your game or toy will develop and describe how it will help.
- Next, observe a baby playing with the game or toy and record a detailed observation.
- Did the baby react as you would expect for a baby of this age and stage of development?

A secret mirror table

Mirrors are a good way to promote visual awareness: they catch the light and reflect different colours, and babies can also see their own movements reflected.

- Stick a few mirror tiles securely to the underside of a low table.

- Place the baby underneath the table so that she or he can look up into the mirror tiles. Check that there is enough light.

- Try to provide a contrasting image – for instance, if the baby's clothing is pale, place the baby on a dark sheet.

Safety point

Before placing the baby on the floor, make sure that there are no draughts.

5 Six months

By 6 months, babies are able to reach for and grab things with both hands. They extend their exploration by using their hands to touch, stroke and pat. Most toys are transferred to the mouth.

They love to imitate sounds and enjoy babbling.

They continue to find other people fascinating, but are wary of strangers.

Physical development

Gross motor skills

At about 6 months, babies:

- if lying on their back can roll over onto their stomach

- if lying on their stomach can lift their head and chest, supporting themselves on their arms and hands

 See clip 3 on DVD

▲ Using the hands and arms for support

▲ Bearing most of the weight

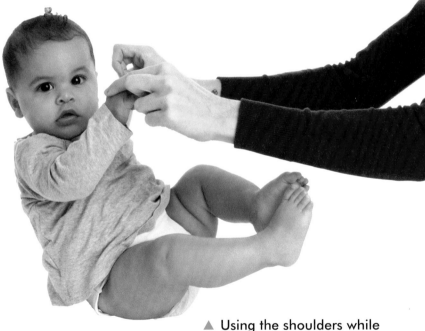

▲ Using the shoulders while moving to a sitting position

- can use their shoulders to pull themselves into a sitting position

- can bear almost all their own weight

- when held standing, do so with a straight back

- when held sitting, do so with a straight back

- when held on the floor, bounce their feet up and down
- lift their legs into a vertical position and grasp one or both feet with their hands
- kick vigorously with their legs alternating
- move their arms purposefully and hold them up, indicating a wish to be lifted
- change the angle of their body to reach out for an object.

▲ Sitting with a straight back – with support if necessary

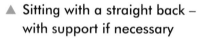

◄ Grasping a foot with the hands

Fine motor skills

At about 6 months, babies:
- reach and grab when a small toy is offered
- use their whole hand (palmar grasp) to pass a toy from one hand to the other
- poke at small objects with their index finger
- explore objects by putting them in their mouth.

 See clip 4 on DVD

▶ Using a palmar grasp

Sensory development

At about 6 months, babies:

- adjust their position to see objects

- are visually very alert, and follow another child's or an adult's activities across the room with increased alertness

- turn towards the source when they hear sounds at ear level.

Cognitive development

▲ Exploring objects with the mouth

At about 6 months, babies:

- understand the meaning of words such as 'bye-bye', 'mama' or 'dada'

- understand objects and know what to expect of them – given a can that makes a noise, for instance, they will test it for other unexpected behaviour

- turn immediately when they hear their mother's or main carer's voice at a distance

- show some understanding of the emotional state of their mother's or main carer's voice

- understand 'up' and 'down' and make appropriate gestures, such as raising their arms to be picked up.

Communication and language development

At about 6 months, babies:

- babble spontaneously, first using monosyllables, such as 'ga, ga', and then double syllables, such as 'goo-ga', and later combining more syllables
- talk to themselves in a tuneful, sing-song voice
- squeal with delight.

Personal, emotional and social development

At about 6 months, babies:

- manage to feed themselves using their fingers
- offer toys to others
- are more wary of strangers
- show distress when their mother leaves
- are more aware of other people's feelings, crying if a sibling cries, for example, or laughing when others do – this is called *recognising an emotion*; it does not mean that they are really feeling that emotion.

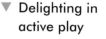

▼ Delighting in active play

Play

At about 6 months, babies:

- show delight in response to active play
- enjoy playing with stacking beakers and bricks
- love to explore objects with both their hands and their mouth
- play with a rolling ball when in a sitting position.

Promoting development

- Encourage confidence and balance by placing toys around the sitting baby.
- Provide rattles and toys that can be hung over the cot – these encourage the baby to reach and grab.
- Encourage mobility by placing toys just out of the baby's reach.
- Provide toys that babies may safely transfer to their mouth.
- Build a tower of bricks with the baby, and share the delight when it topples over.
- Look at picture books together.
- Encourage the baby to point at objects with you.
- Talk about everyday things.
- Widen the baby's experience, for example by going on outings that include animals.
- Imitate animal sounds and encourage the baby to copy you.
- Allow plenty of time for play. Provide simple musical instruments such as a xylophone or a wooden spoon and saucepan.
- Use a mirror to develop the baby's recognition of herself or himself.
- Provide suction toys on tabletops.
- Sing nursery rhymes and lullabies.
- Provide cardboard boxes that the baby can put things into and take things out of.

Safety points

- Make sure that all furniture is stable and has no sharp corners.
- Always supervise a baby when trying finger foods or at mealtimes.
- Always supervise water play.

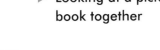

▶ Looking at a picture book together

Activities

Actionrh ymes

Action rhymes promote memory and listening skills. Babies quickly learn to anticipate the next phrase of the rhyme and its associated action.

Two popular rhymes to try with a young baby are 'This Little Piggy' and 'Pat-a-Cake'.

| This Little Piggy

This little piggy went to market

This little piggy stayed at home

This little piggy had roast beef

This little piggy had none

And this little piggy

Went wee wee wee all the way home.

Count the first five lines of the rhyme on the baby's toes, then on the last line run your hand up the baby's leg to tickle her or his tummy.

2 Pat-a-Cake

Pat-a-cake, pat-a-cake, baker's man

Bake me a cake as fast as you can

Pat it and prick it and mark it with 'B'

And put it in the oven for baby and me.

Clap your hands in time to the rhythm of the song and encourage the baby to clap along with you.

Takingturns

Try a simple game of give-and-take with the baby.
This will encourage the skill of being able to let go
of an object, as well as promoting the concept of
turn-taking.

The following is just one way of doing this:

1 Seat the baby safely, supported by cushions or in
a high chair.

2 Pass the baby a toy that can be grasped with
both hands, such as a soft ball or a rattle.

3 Ask the baby: 'Please give me the toy' (or ball, or
whatever it is) and hold out your hands to
receive it.

4 Then pass the toy back to the baby, saying: 'You
can have it back now – here you are.'

Throughout the game, encourage the baby to pass
the object from one hand to another – by showing
how you do this – before passing it to you. This will
increase her or his manipulative skills.

 Observation point

At this stage of development, there is plenty to observe.
You could focus on:
- fine motor skills – noting the way babies use their
hands when handling objects and whether they pass the
object from one hand to another
- play – observing, for example, the way a baby plays
with a cardboard box: does he or she use it to put things
into and take things out of, or to wear as a hat?
- taking turns – for example, observing the baby's
understanding of the concept of turn-taking and also
his or her ability to let go voluntarily of an object when
playing the Taking turns game above.

6 Nine months

By 9 months babies enjoy exploring their environment by crawling or shuffling on their bottoms.

They often bounce in time to music and take pleasure in songs and action rhymes. They can sit, lean forward and pull objects towards them.

Babies understand their daily routine and like to imitate adult speech and gestures.

Physical development

Gross motor skills

At about 9 months, babies:

- can maintain a sitting position with a straight back
- can sit unsupported for up to 15 minutes
- turn their body to look sideways when stretching out to pick up a toy from the floor
- pull themselves to a standing position but are unable to lower themselves and tend to fall backwards with a bump
- stand holding on to furniture

▲ Sitting alone playing with toy

▲ Attempting to crawl

See clip 5 on DVD

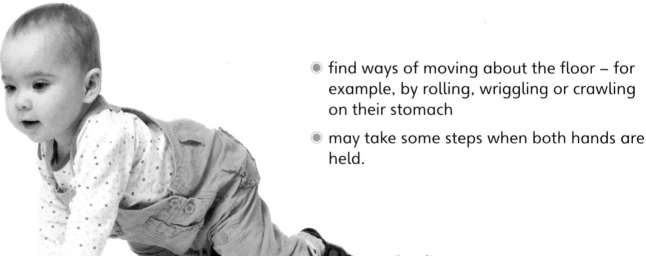

- find ways of moving about the floor – for example, by rolling, wriggling or crawling on their stomach
- may take some steps when both hands are held.

◄ Crawling

Fine motor skills

At about 9 months, babies:

- manipulate toys by passing them from one hand to the other
- can grasp objects between finger and thumb in a pincer grasp
- can release a toy from their grasp by dropping it, but cannot yet put it down voluntarily
- move arms up and down together when excited.

Cognitive development

At about 9 months, babies:

- can judge the size of an object up to 60 cm (2 feet) away
- look in the correct direction for fallen toys
- watch a toy being hidden and then look for it – this shows that they know that an object can exist even when it is no longer in sight (object permanence, s ee also page 175 in Chapter 19)
- recognise familiar pictures
- understand their daily routine and will follow simple instructions such as 'Kiss teddy'.

▲ Grasping an object using a pincer grasp

See clip 6 on DVD

▲ Hiding an object...   ▲ ...looking for it   ▲ ...and 'finding' it again

Communication and language development

At about 9 months, babies:

- use an increasing variety of intonation when babbling
- enjoy communicating with sounds
- imitate adult sounds, like a cough or a 'brrr' noise
- understand and obey the command 'no'
- know general characteristics of their language – they will not respond to a foreign language.

Personal, emotional and social development

At about 9 months, babies:

- enjoy songs and action rhymes
- still prefer to be near to a familiar adult
- play alone for long periods
- show definite likes and dislikes at meals and at bedtimes
- often need to have a comfort object, such as a blanket or a favourite teddy
- still take everything to the mouth
- may drink from a cup with help
- enjoy pointing at objects.

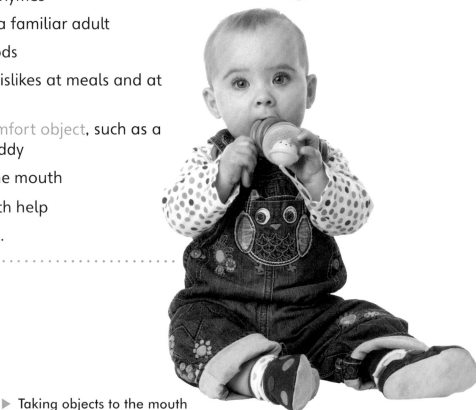

See clip 7 on DVD

See clip 8 on DVD

▶ Taking objects to the mouth

46

Play

At about 9 months, babies:

- play alone for long periods
- enjoy making noises by banging toys
- like to play with empty cardboard boxes.

▲ Playing alone

Promoting development

- Allow plenty of time for play.
- Encourage mobility by placing toys just out of reach.
- Provide small objects for babies to pick up – choose objects that are safe when chewed, such as pieces of biscuit – but always supervise them.
- Provide bath toys, such as beakers, sponges and funnels.
- Provide picture books for babies to explore.
- Provide stacking and nesting toys.
- Play peek-a-boo games, and hide-and-seek.
- Roll balls for the baby to bring or roll back to you.
- Encourage self-feeding and tolerate messes.
- Talk constantly to babies and continue with rhymes and action songs.

Safety points ⚠

- Always supervise eating and drinking. Never leave babies alone with finger foods such as bananas, carrots or cheese.
- Use childproof containers for tablets and vitamins. Ensure that the containers are closed properly.
- Use a locked cupboard for storing dangerous household chemicals such as bleach, disinfectant and white spirit.

▲ Exploring a picture book

Activities

A game of hide-and-seek

1 Choose one of the baby's favourite playthings – perhaps a small soft toy or rattle.

2 Place the baby in a sitting position or lying on his or her stomach.

3 While the baby is watching, place the toy in full view and within easy reach. The baby may reach for the object.

4 Still in full view of the baby, partly cover the toy with a cloth so that only part of it is visible. Again, the baby may reach for the toy.

5 While the baby is reaching for the toy, cover the toy completely with the cloth. Does the baby continue to reach for it?

6 While the baby is still interested in the toy, and again in full view of the baby, completely cover the toy with the cloth once more. Notice whether the baby tries to pull the cloth away or to search for the toy in some way.

 Observation point

Games of hide-and-seek indicate whether the baby has developed the concept of object permanence. You could explore this in a child observation. You will need to find a baby aged between six months and a year whose parent is happy for you to try this activity.

- Follow the procedure outlined in the activity. At each stage, note whether the baby reaches for the toy.
- Write up the results of the activity in the form of an observation.
- If possible, compare this observation with observations of other children.

Research shows that step 4 – continuing to reach for the partly covered toy – is typically experienced at about six months; step 5 at about seven months; and step 6 at about eight months.

7 Twelve months

The way babies view their world changes dramatically as they become more mobile, crawling rapidly or cruising along and using the furniture for support.

At 12 months they are usually still shy with strangers. Often they have a favourite comfort object, such as a teddy or a cloth.

Language develops into conversation, with increasing intonation, although there are very few recognisable words.

They are developing their own sense of identity.

Physical development

Gross motor skills

At about 12 months, babies:

- can rise to a sitting position from lying down
- can rise to standing without help from furniture or people
- can stand alone for a few moments
- can crawl on their hands and knees, bottom-shuffle, or use their hands and feet to move rapidly about the floor (bear-walking)
- can cruise along using furniture as a support
- can probably walk alone, with their feet wide apart and their arms raised to maintain balance – or walk with one hand held.

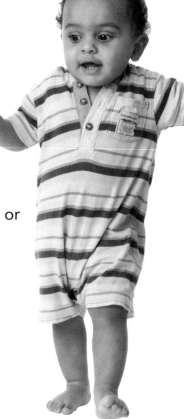

▲ Walking with one hand held

By 13 months, babies:

- can often walk (about 50 per cent of babies walk by this age) but tend to fall over frequently and sit down rather suddenly.

By 15 months, babies:

- crawl upstairs safely and may come downstairs backwards
- are generally able to walk alone
- kneel without support.

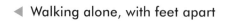

◄ Walking alone, with feet apart

Fine motor skills

At about 12 months, babies:

- can pick up small objects with a fine pincer grasp, between the thumb and the tip of the index finger
- can point with the index finger at objects of interest
- can release a small object into someone's hand
- can hold a crayon in a palmar grasp and turn several pages of a book at once
- show a preference for one hand over the other but use either
- drop and throw toys deliberately and look to see where they have fallen
- build with a few bricks and arrange toys on the floor.

By 15 months, babies:

- can put small objects into a bottle
- can grasp a crayon with either hand in a palmar grasp and imitate to-and-fro scribble
- may build a tower of two cubes after this has been demonstrated.

Sensoryd evelopment

At about 12 months, babies:

- can see almost as well as an adult – their visual memory is very good: they may find things that an adult has mislaid
- know and respond immediately to their own name, and recognise familiar sounds and voices
- stroke, pat and turn objects in their hands and recognise familiar objects by touch alone
- discriminate between different foods by taste and show a preference for sweet, salty and fatty flavours
- often enjoy watching television.

See clip 9 on DVD

▲ Showing a preference for one hand over the other

See clip 10 on DVD

▼ Turning in response to her own name

By 15 months, babies:

- demand objects out of reach by pointing with their index finger

- point to familiar people, animals or toys when requested.

Cognitive development

At about 12 months, babies:

- use trial-and-error methods to learn about objects

- understand simple instructions associated with a gesture, such as 'come to Daddy', 'clap hands' and 'wave bye-bye'

- both point and look to where others point, which implies some understanding of how others see and think.

Communication and language development

At about 12 months, babies:

- speak two to six or more recognisable words and show that they understand many more – babbling has developed into a much more speech-like form, with increased intonation

- hand objects to adults when asked and begin to treat objects in an appropriate way, for example, cuddle a teddy but use a hairbrush.

- Deaf babies stop babbling at around the age of 12 months because they begin to learn the special manual gestures of sign language.

◀ Cuddling a teddy

By 15 months, babies:

- understand the names of various parts of the body
- identify pictures of a few named objects
- understand 'no', 'show me' and 'look'
- watch where objects fall, and can seek out a hidden toy
- move one object to reach another that was hidden from view.

▲ Seeing a toy and a beaker together...

▲ ...recognising that the hidden toy may be with the beaker...

◀ ...and finding the toy

Personal, emotional and social development

At about 12 months, babies:

- are emotionally labile – that is, they are likely to have fluctuating moods
- are closely dependent upon an adult's reassuring presence
- often want a comfort object, such as a teddy or a piece of cloth
- are still shy with strangers
- are affectionate towards familiar people
- enjoy socialising at mealtimes, joining in conversations while mastering the task of self-feeding
- help with daily routines, such as getting washed and dressed
- play pat-a-cake and wave goodbye, both spontaneously and on request.

By 15 months, babies:

- repeatedly throw objects to the floor in play or rejection (this is known as casting)
- carry dolls or teddies by their limbs, hair or clothing.

Play

At about 12 months, babies:

- enjoy playing with bricks, and with containers – they put toys into them and then take them out
- love to play with toys that they can move along with their feet
- enjoy looking at picture books.

Promoting development

- Provide a wheeled push-and-pull toy to promote confidence in walking.
- Provide stacking toys and bricks.
- Read picture books with simple rhymes.
- Arrange a corner of the kitchen or garden for messy play. Encourage the use of water, play dough or paint.
- Encourage skills of creativity by providing thick crayons and paint brushes and large sheets of paper (such as wall lining paper).
- Play simple games with the baby that involve action and taking turns, such as the *Hand sandwich* game.

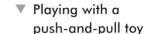

▼ Playing with a push-and-pull toy

- Join in games of *Let's pretend* to encourage skills of imagination – for example, pretending to be animals or to drive a bus.

- Encourage role-play games of make-believe – for example, pretending to be a doctor, a vet or a superhero.

- Talk to the baby about everyday activities, but always allow time for a response.

- Provide an interesting, varied environment, which contains pictures, music, books and food, all of which stimulate the senses.

- Consider attending a mother-and-toddler group or a similar group.

Safety points

- As babies become more mobile, you need to be vigilant at all times. This is a very high-risk age for accidents.

- Always supervise sand and water play.

- Use safety equipment, such as safety catches for cupboards and stair gates, ideally at both the top and bottom of stairs.

Activities

A pull-along snake

Once a child is walking with confidence, you could make a colourful pull-along toy. Brightly painted cotton reels threaded onto soft cord or string make an attractive snake for children to pull along. Alternatively, you could thread together plastic hair rollers or large round beads.

1 Paint 10–12 large cotton reels in bright colours, using lead-free paint.

2 Thread the reels onto a cord, about 0.75 m (20 inches) long.

3 Knot the cord to ensure that the reels are about 0.5 cm (¼ inch) apart so that the snake will twist and turn when pulled.

4 Use a large oval bead to make the snake's head. Paint an eye on each side.

5 Use small wooden or plastic beads to make an easy-to-grip handle.

This activity promotes the motor skills of balance and co-ordination, and encourages children to become aware of their ability to control their own environment.

Choosing toys for babies

Visit a toyshop and look at the range of toys for babies under 18 months old. Make a list – you could group the toys and activities under two headings:

● toys that will strengthen muscles and improve co-ordination skills

● toys that will particularly stimulate the senses of touch, hearing and sight.

Check the safety symbols shown on the toys.

If you were asked to suggest toys and activities for a baby with visual impairment, what specific toys could you suggest? Why?

 Observation point

Observe a child who has recently learned to walk. Include the following in your observation:
- how the child begins to walk – does he or she stand first?
- the gait of the child: that is, does the child appear bow-legged (this is normal at first!) and do they walk with legs wide apart?
- if – and how often – the child reaches out for support
- how often the child suddenly sits down.

This need only be a short observation, but should be focused completely on the walking activity.

8 Eighteen months

Children of 18 months enjoy being able to walk well and can climb up and down stairs with help.

They can pick up small objects with a delicate pincer grasp and show a preference for using one hand.

They enjoy simple picture books and can understand and obey simple commands.

Children have an increasing desire for independence and are developing a recognisable character and personality of their own.

Physical development

Gross motor skills

At about 18 months, children:

- can walk steadily and stop safely, without sitting down suddenly
- can climb forward into an adult chair and then turn around and sit
- can kneel upright without support
- can squat to pick up or move a toy
- can move without support from a squatting position to standing

▲ Walking steadily, even when carrying a toy

▲ Climbing onto an adult chair....

 See clip 11 on DVD

▲ ....and turning round to sit on it

- can climb up and down stairs if their hand is held or using a rail for balance – they put two feet on each step before moving on to the next step
- can crawl backwards (on the stomach) down stairs alone
- can run steadily but are unable to avoid obstacles in their path.

▲ Moving from squatting to standing

Fine motor skills: gross manipulative skills

At about 18 months, children:

- can point to known objects
- can build a tower of three or more bricks.

▲ Building a tower of bricks

Fine motor skills: fine manipulative skills

At about 18 months, children:

- can use a delicate pincer grasp to pick up very small objects
- can use a spoon when feeding themselves
- can hold a pencil in their whole hand or between the thumb and the first two fingers (this is called the primitive tripod grasp)
- can scribble to and fro with a pencil
- can thread large beads onto a lace or string
- can control their wrist movement to manipulate objects
- can remove small objects from a bottle by turning it upside down.

See clip 12 on DVD

▲ Using a primitive tripod grasp

Sensorydev elopment

At about 18 months, children:

- recognise familiar people at a distance
- realise that they are looking at themselves in the mirror
- no longer take everything to their mouths to explore it.

Cognitive development

At about 18 months, children:

- know the names of parts of their bodies and can point to them when asked
- recognise that people may have different desires (younger babies assume that everyone feels the same as they do).

Communication and language development

At about 18 months, children:

- use 6–40 recognisable words and understand many more (the word most often used is 'no'!)
- echo the last part of what others say (echolalia)
- over-extend words or signs, giving them several meanings (holophrase) – for example, 'cat' may be used to refer to all animals, not just cats
- begin waving their arms up and down, meaning 'start again', 'more' or 'I like it'
- use gestures alongside words
- indicate desire by pointing, urgent vocalisations or words
- obey simple instructions such as 'Shut the door' and respond to simple questions such as 'Where's the pussy-cat?'
- enjoy trying to sing, as well as listening to songs and rhymes
- refer to themselves by name.

Personal, emotional and social development

At about 18 months, children:

- remember where objects belong (this reflects an increase in long-term memory)

- play contentedly alone (solitary play) but prefer to be near a familiar adult or sibling

- are eager to be independent, for example to dress themselves ('Me do it!')

- are aware that others are fearful or anxious for them as they climb on or off chairs etc.

- alternate between clinging and resistance

- may easily become frustrated, with occasional temper tantrums

- may indicate toilet needs by restlessness or words

- can follow and enjoy stories and rhymes that include repetition.

▲ Playing contentedly alone

 See clip 13 on DVD

Play

At about 18 months, children:

- like things that screw and unscrew

- enjoy posting objects into boxes, as when posting letters

- like paints and crayons

- enjoy sand and water play, and associated toys

- like to play matching and sorting games, for example stacking beakers

- enjoy simple jigsaw puzzles

- love puppet play and action rhymes.

▲ Playing with a glove puppet

Promoting development

- Continue to provide walker trucks, pull-along animals and the like.

- Encourage play with messy materials, such as sand, water and play dough.

- Provide low, stable furniture to climb on.

- Provide pop-up toys, stacking toys and hammer-and-peg toys, which develop hand–eye co-ordination skills.

- Provide balls to roll, kick or throw.

- Provide toys that encourage make-believe play and language skills, such as simple puppets, dressing-up clothes or toy telephones.

- Use action rhymes and singing games to promote conversation and confidence. Play with other children will help, too.

- Provide bath toys, such as simple beakers, sprinkling toys and waterproof books.

- Use finger-paints and wax crayons to encourage creative skills.

- Provide picture books, and encourage children to turn the pages and to identify details in the pictures.

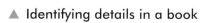

▲ Identifying details in a book

See clip 14 on DVD

Safety points ⚠

- Always supervise children in the bath. Never leave a child alone in the bath, even for a few minutes.
- When children are climbing or playing outside, be aware of dangers such as sharp objects, litter or unfenced ponds.

Activities

A treasure basket

Make a treasure basket for a child aged 18 months.

1 Use a strong, shallow cardboard box, an old solid wooden drawer or a wicker basket.

2 Check that there are no staples, splinters or jagged edges.

3 Select a variety of interesting objects (about 10–15 in all) that will stimulate each of the child's senses – objects with different shapes, weights, colours and textures. You may also be able to include objects that have a distinctive smell, such as a small empty perfume bottle or a lavender bag.

➡

Observation point

You could use this activity for a child observation.

1 Sit to one side and observe the child playing alone with the contents of the treasure chest. Write a detailed, timed observation of the activity, including the following points:

- *what the child does with each object*
- *how long he or she plays with each object*
- *what expressions or sounds he or she makes*
- *how involved he or she is in the activity.*

2 Evaluate the activity in terms of its value to the child's overall development and enjoyment.

3 What would you change if you were to repeat the activity?

◀ Using a treasure basket

Puppetp lay

Make two simple finger puppets: one (large) for you, and the other (slightly smaller) for the child.

I   Using a square of felt, cut and stick or sew a small cap shape to fit over the finger. Decorate it with hair (wool) and a face.

2   Play a game in which the child copies your actions, such as:

My little man bows down

My little man turns round

My little man jumps up and down

And makes a funny sound – BOO!

This activity promotes manipulative skills, social and language development and the development of imagination.

9 Two years

By 2 years, children can run, jump, kick, and use words as well as actions to express themselves.

They are curious and impulsive explorers of their environment and want to be as independent as possible. They are starting to play independently.

Children easily become frustrated when they cannot express themselves or are prevented from doing something they want to do.

They may show strong emotions in temper tantrums or bursting into tears – the classic 'terrible twos'. They are also affected by the emotions of others and will laugh or cry in sympathy.

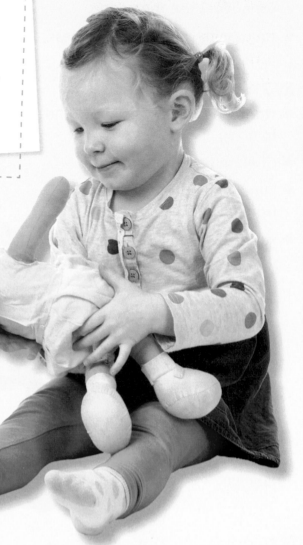

Physical development

Gross motor skills

From the age of 2, children:

- can run safely, avoiding obstacles and are very mobile
- can climb up onto furniture
- can throw a ball overarm, but cannot yet catch a ball
- push and pull large, wheeled toys
- walk up and down stairs, usually putting both feet on each step
- walk into a large ball when attempting to kick it
- sit on a tricycle and propel it with their feet – they cannot yet use the pedals
- squat with complete steadiness.

By 2½ years, children:

- stand on tiptoe when shown how to do so
- climb nursery apparatus
- jump with both feet together from a low step
- kick a large ball, but gently and lopsidedly.

▲ Preparing to throw a ball overarm

◄ Riding a tricycle – propelling it with the feet

Fine motor skills

From the age of 2, children:

- draw circles, lines and dots using their preferred hand
- pick up tiny objects using a fine pincer grasp
- can build a tower of six or more blocks, using a longer concentration span
- enjoy picture books and turn the pages singly
- can copy a vertical line and sometimes a 'V' shape with a pencil
- can drink from a cup with fewer spills, and manage scooping with a spoon at mealtimes.

By 2½ years, children:

- eat skilfully with a spoon and may use a fork
- can hold a pencil in their preferred hand, with an improved tripod grasp
- can build a tower of seven or more cubes, using their preferred hand
- can imitate a horizontal line, a circle, a 'T' and a 'V' with a pencil.

▲ Attempting to kick a large ball

Sensoryd evelopment

From the age of 2, children:

- recognise familiar people in photographs after being shown them once, but do not yet recognise themselves in photographs
- listen to general conversation with interest.

By 2½ years, children:

- recognise themselves in photos
- recognise minute details in picture books.

▶ Drinking confidently from a cup
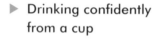

Cognitive development

From the age of 2, children:

- are particularly interested in the names of people and objects

- are beginning to understand the consequences of their own actions and those of others, for example when something falls over or breaks

- provide comfort when other babies cry – empathy requires a deep knowledge of other minds (younger babies cry when others cry).

Communication and language development

From the age of 2, children:

- talk to themselves often, but may not always be understood by others

- now speak over 200 words, and accumulate new words very rapidly

- understand many more words than they can speak (possibly over a thousand)

- talk about an absent object when reminded of it – seeing an empty plate, for instance, they may say 'biscuit'

- often omit opening or closing consonants, so 'bus' may become 'us', or 'coat' become 'coa'

- use phrases as telegraphic speech (or telegraphese)– for example, 'daddy-car' might mean a number of different things, including 'Daddy's in his car', 'I want to go in Daddy's car' or 'Daddy's car is outside'

See clip 15 on DVD

- spend a great deal of time in naming things and what they do, such as 'chair' or 'step' and 'up'
- follow simple instructions and requests, such as 'Please bring me the book'
- want to share songs, conversations and finger-rhymes more and more.

By 2½ years, children:
- know their full name
- still repeat words spoken to them (echolalia)
- continually ask questions beginning 'What... ?' or 'Who... ?'
- use the pronouns 'I', 'me' and 'you' correctly
- talk audibly and intelligibly to themselves when playing
- can say a few nursery rhymes.

Personal, emotional and social development

From the age of 2, children:
- are beginning to express how they feel
- are impulsive and curious about their environment
- are eager to try out new experiences
- may be clingy and dependent at times and self-reliant and independent at others
- often feel frustrated when unable to express themselves – about half of 2-year-old children have tantrums on a more or less daily basis
- can dress themselves independently
- often like to help others, but not when doing so conflicts with their own desires.

By 2½ years, children:

- may be dry through the night (but there is wide variation)
- are emotionally still very dependent on an adult
- may go to the toilet independently but may need sensitive help with pulling their pants up
- play more with other children but may not share their toys with them.

 See clip 16 on DVD

Play

From the age of 2, children:

- love physical games, including running, jumping and climbing
- like to build with construction toys
- engage in more sustained role-play, such as putting dolls to bed or driving a car
- often play alone (solitary play) or watch other children playing (spectator play)

▼ Spectator play

- understand the concept of 'one' and 'lots'
- count by rote up to ten, but do not appreciate quantity beyond two or three
- can control their attention, choosing to stop an activity and return to it without much difficulty.

Communication and language development

From the age of 3, children:

- use personal pronouns and plurals correctly and can give their own name and sex, and sometimes age
- carry on simple conversations, often missing link words such as 'the' and 'is'
- learn to speak more than one language if they hear more than one language spoken around them as they grow
- still talk to themselves when playing
- enjoy listening to and making music.

 See clip 19 on DVD

Personal, emotional and social development

From the age of 3, children:

- like to do things unaided
- enjoy family mealtimes
- can think about things from someone else's point of view
- show affection for younger siblings
- manage to use the lavatory independently and are often dry through the night (though this is variable between children and from day to day with a given child)

- enjoy helping adults, as in tidying up
- are willing to share toys with other children and are beginning to take turns when playing

See clip 20 on DVD

- often develop fears, for example of the dark, as they become capable of pretending and imagining
- are becoming aware of being male or female (are developing a gender role)
- make friends and are interested in having friends.

Moral and spiritual development

From the age of 3, children:
- are beginning to develop the concept of being helpful
- believe that all rules are fixed and unchallengeable – for example, if told that coats must be worn when playing outside, they accept this without question.

Play

From the age of 3, children:
- like to ride tricycles and play outdoors
- enjoy simple craft activities, for example with scissors and beads, and playing with dough
- join in active pretend play with other children

See clip 21 on DVD

- enjoy playing on the floor with bricks, boxes, trains and dolls, both alone and with others
- like jigsaw puzzles and making models.

Promoting development

- Provide a wide variety of playthings – balls for throwing and catching, sand, jigsaw puzzles and so on.

- Encourage play with other children.

- Provide a variety of art and craft activities: thick crayons, stubby paintbrushes, paper, paint and dough for modelling or play cooking.

- Talk to children often and read to them, to encourage the development of language.

- Encourage children to use their fingers to help count to ten. They will begin to learn that five and five make ten and they can fold down four fingers and see that there are six fingers still up.

- Encourage swimming and trips to the park. Children may even enjoy longer walks.

- Promote independence by teaching children how to look after and put away their own clothes and toys.

- Provide toys for water play, perhaps in the bath or paddling pool.

- Let them help you cook – you could make some biscuits.

- Encourage visits to the library and story times.

- Play simple matching and sorting games with them, such as lotto.

Safety points

- During cookery activities, never let the child use the oven or handle hot liquids.
- Make sure that any spills are wiped up promptly.
- If cooking within a nursery setting, keep the maximum number of children to four.
- Always supervise water play.

◀ Playing with dough

Watching TV, videos, DVDs

- Limit the amount of TV children watch; 10–15 minute periods are about right for this age group.

- Be selective: prepare children for a programme or video that is due to start and switch the TV off after the programme has finished.

- Choose programmes that are fairly slow-paced and which emphasise interactivity; ones that inspire children to make sounds or to sing and dance are good.

- Avoid busy cartoon adventures, which can be very noisy.

- Watch TV with children where possible, so that you are there to explain what is happening and to encourage questions.

- Extend the programme's content with activities or books; for example, if a programme such as *Bob the Builder* or *Peppa Pig* explores the concept of number, follow through with a counting song.

Using computers

Computer use for most children under age 3 does not have meaning for the child. See ICT Guidelines for children aged 3 to 5 years on page 98.

▲ Making music together

Activities

Making musical instruments

You can help children to make a range of percussive (beating) and shaking instruments.

1 Collect together tins to beat with wooden spoons, saucepan lids to clash together, and securely closed jars containing pasta or pulses to shake.

2 Look for anything that children can safely manipulate and that makes an interesting sound.

Making music using the voice

The voice is the most natural musical instrument there is. As well as speaking and singing with it, you can make a whole range of different sounds. This activity encourages experimentation and, with the help of a tape recorder, allows children to find out what they can do with their voice.

1 You need a portable tape recorder with a built-in microphone.

2 If the child is not already familiar with it, demonstrate the workings of the tape recorder.

3 You could start off with the child singing a favourite song or rhyme, then play the tape back to hear how it sounds. You could talk about the different sounds on the tape and begin to describe them.

4 Try the following ideas:

- speak in a very high and very low voice
- speak very fast or very slowly
- whisper very quietly – close to the microphone
- shout – a long way from the microphone!
- make animal noises
- hum a tune.

Observation points

- Make a detailed observation of the activity.
- Outline the possible benefits to the child and write an evaluation.

Picturelo tto

You can buy a ready-made lotto game, but you might enjoy making your own.

1 Find some suitable illustrations for a simple picture lotto game.

2 Make your picture lotto game by pasting three sets of six or more coloured pictures of toys or household objects onto three large pieces of card. Cut round the pictures on two of the cards, leaving one as your playing board.

3 To play lotto, simply fill up the playing board by turning over cards that match.

Games such as lotto encourage the concept of one-to-one correspondence, which is vital for the child's understanding of number.

◀ Playing picture lotto

11 Four years

At 4 years of age, children are quite capable and independent.

They walk with swinging steps, almost like an adult's, and like to hop and jump.

Children are fascinated by cause and effect and their increasing mastery of language prompts them to ask questions about the way things work in the world.

Physical development

Gross motor skills

From the age of 4, children:

- have developed a good sense of balance and may be able to walk along a line

- can stand, walk and run on tiptoe

▲ Moving with a good sense of balance

◀ Bouncing a ball

- can catch, kick, throw and bounce a ball
- bend at the waist to pick up objects from the floor
- enjoy climbing trees and on frames
- run up and down stairs, one foot per step
- can ride a tricycle with skill and make sharp turns easily.

▲ Running on tiptoe

Fine motor skills

From the age of 4, children:

- can build a tower of ten or more cubes
- can copy a building pattern using six bricks or more

 See clip 22 on DVD

▲ Copying a building pattern
with more than six bricks

- are able to thread small beads on a lace
- hold and use a pencil or pen in an adult fashion
- can draw on request a figure that resembles a person, showing head, legs and body
- can copy the letters 'X', 'V', 'H', 'T' and 'O'
- can spread their hand, and can bring their thumbs into opposition with each finger in turn.

◀ Holding a pen in
an adult fashion

Sensory development

From the age of 4, children:

- match and name primary colours
- listen to long stories with attention.

▶ Sharing a picture book

Cognitive development

From the age of 4, children:

- enjoy counting up to 20 by rote and understand the concept of number up to three
- talk about things in the past and the future
- can sort objects into groups
- have increased memory skills – for example, they can remember a particular event, such as when their grandparents visited several months previously
- can give reasons and solve problems
- include more detail in their drawings, such as adding hands and fingers to drawings of people
- often confuse fact with fiction.

Communication and language development

From the age of 4, children:

- talk fluently, asking questions ('Why... ?', 'When... ?', 'How... ?') and understanding the answers

- can repeat nursery rhymes and songs, with very few errors

- can state their full name and address almost correctly

- tell long stories, sometimes confusing fact and fantasy

- enjoy jokes and plays on words

- may begin to recognise patterns in the way words are formed and apply these consistently, unaware that many common words have irregular forms – for example, as the past tense is often made by adding '-ed' ('I walk' becomes 'I walked'), children may say 'I runned' or 'I goed' instead of 'I ran' or 'I went'.

See clip 23 on DVD

Personal, emotional and social development

From the age of 4, children:

- can eat skilfully with a spoon and a fork

- can wash and dry their hands, and brush their teeth

- can undress and dress themselves, except for laces, ties and back buttons

- often show sensitivity to others

- show a sense of humour, both in talk and in activities

- like to be independent and are strongly self-willed

- like to be with other children.

See clip 24 on DVD

▶ Dressing unaided

Moral and spiritual development

From the age of 4, children:

- understand the needs of others and the need to share and take turns

- try to work out what is right and what is wrong in behaviour.

Play

From the age of 4, children:

- act out puppet shows and scenes they have seen on television

- play elaborate role-play games with others

- enjoy imaginative play, which helps them to cope with strong emotions.

Promoting development

- Provide children with plenty of opportunities for exercise.

- Play party games, such as musical statues, to foster the ideas of winning, losing and co-operation.

- Encourage children to use rope swings and climbing frames.

- Encourage play with small construction toys, jigsaw puzzles and board games.

- Provide art and craft materials for painting, printing, and gluing and sticking activities.

- Encourage sand and water play, and play with dough or modelling clay.

- Talk often with children. Repeat favourite stories and encourage them to express themselves.

- Visit the library and read books together.

- Look for books and puzzles that help children to categorise and sort objects.

- Play lotto and other matching games such as pairs (pelmanism).

- Display children's paintings around the house – this gives them a feeling of pride in their work.

- Teach children how to dress and undress themselves in preparation for school games lessons.

- Encourage independence when going to the toilet.

- Let children practise using a computer mouse and carrying out simple computer activities.

- Organise visits to parks and farms. Encourage children to draw what they have seen.

- Involve children in caring for pets to encourage a sense of responsibility.

- Provide a box of dressing-up clothes for imaginative play.

- Let children organise their own games with friends, to encourage independence and confidence.

- Try not to rush to help when children are finding an activity difficult – allow them time to master new skills, offering praise and encouragement.

Safety points

- Teach children never to play with sticks or other sharp objects, or to run with a pencil or lolly stick in their mouth.

- Teach children not to eat berries or fungi.

- Educate children about road safety by setting a good example.

Activity

Making a book

Helping children to make a book of their own is a good way of encouraging a liking for books.

One idea is to make a book about the child and about the people and things that mean a lot to her or him. This could include drawings or photographs of:

- family and friends
- toys and favourite things
- birthdays and holidays
- pets and other animals
- favourite foods and games.

The book need not be elaborate; the main idea is to involve the child in the making of it and thereby increase her or his self-esteem. You could buy a scrapbook or a large notebook, or just fold some large sheets of paper in half, punch holes along the fold, and thread some ribbon or cord through them.

Growing mustard and cress

Children will enjoy growing their own plants and discovering how to care for them.

1 Collect some empty eggshells. Give each child a shell and ask them to draw a face on their own shell.

2 Cut a cardboard egg carton into individual pockets. Place one eggshell in each pocket.

3 Pack each shell generously with cotton wool and soak this with water before putting the seeds on top.

4 Water the cotton wool regularly and wait for the green 'hair' to sprout. (This should only take two or three days.)

Observation point

Observe a four year old child – or group of children – during an activity and focus on their communication and language skills. Try to include all aspects of communication, including observation of:
- speech
- facial expression
- body language
- posture
- tone of voice
- actions.

You may choose to use a time sampling method, observing the ways in which your target child communicates in a variety of situations and with different people, including other children and adults.

12 Five years

Children enjoy showing what they can do – hopping, skipping, dancing and playing group ball games.

They have a growing awareness of the world and their language shows this understanding.

Children are learning self-control, including how to wait and how to take turns.

They are completely independent in everyday skills, such as washing, dressing and eating.

Physical development

Gross motor skills

From the age of 5, children:

- have increased agility – they can run and dodge, run lightly on their toes, climb and skip
- show good balance – they can stand on one foot for about ten seconds, and some may ride a bike without stabilisers
- show good co-ordination, playing ball games and dancing rhythmically to music
- can bend at the waist and touch their toes without bending at the knees
- can hop 2–3 m (6–9 feet) forwards on each foot separately
- use a variety of play equipment, including slides, swings and climbing frames.

▲ Bending at the waist and touching the toes

Fine motor skills

From the age of 5, children:

- can use a knife and fork competently, but may still need to have meat cut up for them
- may be able to thread a large-eyed needle and sew with large stitches
- have good control over pencils and paint brushes
- can draw a person with a head, a body, arms, legs, a nose, a mouth and eyes
- can copy elaborate models, such as a four-step model using ten cubes

▶ Drawing a person

- can construct elaborate models using kits (such as Duplo®)

- can copy a square and, at 5½ years, a triangle

- can copy letters 'V', 'T', 'H', 'O', 'X', 'L', 'A', 'C', 'U' and 'Y'

- can count the fingers on one hand using the index finger of the other

- can do jigsaw puzzles with interlocking pieces.

▶ Constructing an elaborate model

Sensoryd evelopment

From the age of 5, children:

- can match ten or twelve colours.

Cognitive development

See clip 25 on DVD

From the age of 5, children:

- produce drawings with good detail – for example, a house with windows, a door, a roof and a chimney

- ask about abstract words (for instance, 'What does "beyond" mean?')

- can give their full name, age and address, and often their birthday

- are interested in reading and writing

- recognise their name and attempt to write it.

Communication and language development

From the age of 5, children:

- talk about the past, present and future, with a good sense of time
- are fluent in their speech and grammatically correct for the most part
- love to be read stories and will then act them out in detail later, either alone or with friends
- enjoy jokes and riddles.

Personal, emotional and social development

From the age of 5, children:

- dress and undress alone, but may have difficulty with shoelaces
- have very definite likes and dislikes, some with little apparent logic – for example, a child might eat carrots when cut into strips but not when cut into rounds
- are able to amuse themselves for longer periods of time, for example looking at a book or watching a DVD
- show sympathy and comfort friends who are hurt
- enjoy caring for pets
- choose their own friends.

Moral and spiritual development

From the age of 5, children:

- understand the social rules of their culture, for example the usual way to greet somebody

- instinctively help other children when they are distressed.

Play

From the age of 5, children:

- enjoy team games and games with rules

- may show a preference for a particular sport or craft activity

- play complicated games on the floor with miniature objects (small-world play)

- play alone or with others, including younger children

- enjoy elaborate pretend play with others.

▼ Enjoying a card game

ICT guidelines for children aged three to five years

Using computers

Computers should supplement – and not replace – activities such as art, sand and water play, music, outdoor exploration, reading stories together or sharing conversations and socialising with other children. Using the computer should be just one of many activity choices for children to explore. For computer activities to be successful with young children, adults should:

- observe the way children use the computer to solve problems
- monitor the amount of time spent at the computer
- avoid telling children what to do next, but be available to help them work out what to do for themselves
- encourage children to work with another child to promote the social skills of turn-taking and sharing
- talk with them about their activities and be on hand to answer questions
- extend and reinforce the learning: this means applying the lessons learned at the computer to other activities, such as games, identifying numbers, shapes or letters or acting out stories from the program.

The software selected must be developmentally appropriate – that is, consistent with how children develop and learn – and should also fit their need to interact with their environment. Software for young children should:

- encourage exploration, imagination and problem-solving
- reflect and build on what children already know
- involve many senses and include sound, music and voice
- be open-ended: it should encourage creativity, language skills, early reading skills and problem-solving, with the child in control of the pace and the direction
- provide equal opportunities for all children; for example, software should be easily adaptable to children who have a hearing or sight problem.

Promoting development

- Provide plenty of outdoor activities.
- Provide stilts to encourage balance and co-ordination – these could be made from old paint cans and strong cord.
- Teach children to ride a two-wheeled bicycle.
- Teach children to swim.
- Encourage non-stereotypical activities, such as boys using skipping ropes and girls playing football.
- Team sports may be provided at school or at clubs such as Beavers, Rainbows and Woodcraft Folk.
- Encourage the use of models, jigsaws, sewing kits and craft activities, as well as drawing and painting.
- Talk to children about past, present and future, to promote language skills.
- Allow children to organise their own games.
- Encourage children to help with simple tasks, such as washing-up or watering plants.
- Set clear boundaries for behaviour, and always explain these to children.

Safety points

- If you have large picture windows, mark them with coloured strips to make it obvious when they are closed.
- When out at dusk or when walking on country roads without pavements, use luminous armbands or light-coloured clothing for children.

▶ Balancing on stilts

Activity

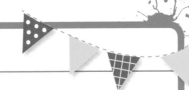

Conservation of number

Conservation is the name for the concept that objects remain the same in fundamental ways, such as in their volume or number, even when there are external changes in their shape or arrangement.

This activity uses plastic bricks but you could also use buttons. The aim of the activity is to see whether the child recognises that the same number of objects remain, even when they have been arranged differently.

1 Make two rows of objects. Check that the child agrees that the two rows contain the same number in each row.

2 Spread one row out to make a longer row. Ask the child which row contains *more* objects.

 See clip 26 on DVD

 Observation point

Jean Piaget (1896–1980) was a psychologist who studied the way in which children develop intellectually. Piaget stated that children under 7 years old would not conserve when presented with the activity above. However, other researchers have found that children as young as 5 or 6 years old are able to understand that objects remain the same, even when arranged differently.

- You could try this simple experiment with several children aged 5, 6 and 7 years old.
- Record your findings in an observation and compare the results from the different age groups.

13 Six years

Children of 6 years are full of curiosity and are developing their own interests.

They are forming new concepts of size, shape, weight and distance.

They are growing towards reading and writing independently, putting words and ideas down on paper and often using invented spelling.

Physical development

Gross motor skills

From the age of 6, children:

- are gaining in both strength and agility; they can jump off apparatus at school with confidence

- can run and jump, and can kick a football up to 6 m (18 feet)

◀ Jumping with confidence

▲ Jumping off apparatus

- can hop easily, with good balance

- can catch and throw balls with accuracy

- can ride a two-wheeled bike, possibly without stabilisers

- can skip in time to music, alternating their feet.

Fine motor skills

From the age of 6, children:

- can build a tower of cubes that is virtually straight
- can hold a pen or pencil in a way similar to that of an adult (the dynamic tripod grasp)
- are able to write a number of letters of similar size
- can write their last name as well as their first name
- may begin to write simple stories.

◀ Hopping with good balance

◀ Building straight towers

See clip 27 on DVD

▲ Using a pen with a dynamic tripod grasp

▲ Writing a name

Cognitive development

From the age of 6, children:

- begin to think in a more co-ordinated way, and can hold more than one point of view at a time

- begin to develop concepts of quantity: length, measurement, distance, area, time, volume, capacity and weight

- are able to distinguish the difference between reality and fantasy, but are often still frightened by supernatural characters in books, on the television and so on

- are interested in basic scientific principles and are beginning to understand, for example, what happens to everyday materials if they are soaked or heated

- are increasingly influenced by cultural conventions in drawing and writing, for example, often combining their own personal symbols with letters from the alphabet

- draw people in detail including, for instance, eyebrows and eyelashes, and buttons and laces on clothes.

▲ Exploring concepts of quantity

Communication and language development

From the age of 6, children:

- can pronounce the majority of the sounds of their own language

- talk fluently and with confidence

- can remember and repeat nursery rhymes and songs

- are steadily developing literacy skills (reading and writing), although the ability to read independently with confidence usually begins between 7 and 9 years of age

- alternate between wanting stories read to them and reading books themselves.

Personal, emotional and social development

From the age of 6, children:

- can carry out simple tasks, such as peeling vegetables, watering plants, hanging up clothes and tidying the contents of drawers

- choose friends mainly because of their personality and interests

See clip 28 on DVD

- can hold a long conversation with another child or an adult, naturally taking turns in speaking and listening

- begin to compare themselves with other people – 'I am like her in that way but different in this way…'

Moral and spiritual development

From the age of 6, children:

- are beginning to develop further concepts, such as forgiveness and fairness.

Play

From the age of 6, children:

- play together with other children (co-operative play)
- assign roles to others in elaborate pretend play and role-play
- role-play situations of which they have no direct experience, but which might happen to them one day, such as getting married or travelling through space to the moon (fantasy play).

 See clip 29 on DVD

Promoting development

- Provide opportunity for vigorous exercise.
- Allow children to try a new activity or sport, such as football, dancing, judo or gymnastics.
- Encourage writing skills by providing lots of examples of things written for different purposes, such as shopping lists, letters and recipes.
- Play memory games with children, such as pairs and dominoes.
- Talk to children about what they have done during the day.
- Encourage children to sort and match objects. Ask them to order things according to more abstract concepts, such as sweetness or preference.
- Try not to correct grammatical mistakes – instead, respond by subtly rephrasing their statement while showing that you have understood them. Thus a child might say, 'A lion is more fiercer than a cat' and you could reply, 'Yes, lions are fiercer than cats'.
- Create a warm, supporting atmosphere during story time at home or at school, with plenty of talk about the story you are reading.

Safety points

Give children clear guidelines about safety. For example:

- never climb a tree without first asking an adult's permission
- never cross a road without an accompanying adult
- never accept anything offered by a stranger
- never, ever go anywhere with a stranger.

Activities

Cookingbi scuits

Making biscuits gives plenty of opportunities for measuring, mixing, rolling out, cutting shapes and decorating.

Get together everything you will need before you begin, so that you do not have to leave children unsupervised. If cooking at school, limit the number of children to four. Follow these guidelines:

- teach children to wash their hands and dry them thoroughly before cooking
- teach them to be very careful when handling knives
- teach them to ask before tasting anything
- clear up any spills immediately.

Here is a basic biscuit recipe:

- 125 g (4 oz) soft margarine or butter
- 125 g (4 oz) sugar (white or brown)
- 250 g (8 oz) plain flour
- 1e gg
- pinch of salt
- grated orange or lemon rind if desired.

▶ Making biscuits

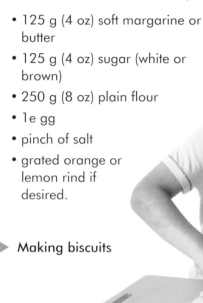

Making the biscuits:

1 Pre-heat the oven (moderate: 190°C, 375°F or gas mark 5).

2 Beat the margarine and sugar together.

3 Beat the egg and add to the mixture.

4 Sift in the flour and the salt (and the grated rind, if used).

5 Mix to form a ball of dough.

6 Roll out the dough to a thickness of 0.5 cm (¼ inch). Cut into shapes.

7 Put the shapes on a greased baking tray and bake them in the middle of the oven for about 15 minutes.

Earlys cience

Try out this simple demonstration of static electricity with a child or a group of children.

1 Stir a little salt and pepper together.

2 Ask the child to separate them using a teaspoon. This, of course, is not possible.

3 Then rub the spoon against a sweater – ideally one made of acrylic or another synthetic fibre. This creates static electricity on the spoon.

4 Simply hold the spoon just above the mixture. Pepper is lighter than salt and the static electricity on the spoon will lift it free.

 Observation point

Make a detailed observation of the activity. Notice the language used by the children and the understanding of concepts that they demonstrate.

14 Seven years

Children at 7 have a well-developed sense of balance and enjoy activities that involve precise movements, such as hopscotch or skipping games.

They are interested in talking, listening, and reading and writing and enjoy games with rules.

They have a clear sense of right and wrong and see friendships as very important.

Physical development

Gross motor skills

From the age of 7, children:

- can hop on either leg and can walk along a thin line with their arms outstretched for balance

- may be expert at riding a two-wheeled bike or using roller skates

- can climb on play apparatus with skill, some managing to climb ropes

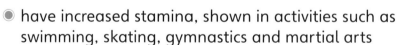

▲ Walking along a narrow line

- have increased stamina, shown in activities such as swimming, skating, gymnastics and martial arts

- are able to control their speed when running and can swerve to avoid collision

- are skilful in catching and throwing a ball, using one hand only.

◀ Catching a ball with one hand

 See clip 30 on DVD

Fine motor skills

From the age of 7, children:

- can build tall, straight towers with cubes
- are more competent in their writing skills – individual letters are more clearly differentiated now, and capital and small letters are in proportion
- begin to use colour in a naturalistic way, for example using a band of green colour at the bottom of the page to represent grass and a band of blue across the top to represent sky
- draw people with heads, bodies, hands, hair, fingers and clothes
- can use a large needle to sew with thread.

Cognitive development

From the age of 7, children:

- are able to conserve number – for example, they know that there are ten sweets whether they are pushed close together or spread apart
- express themselves in speech and writing
- can use a computer mouse and keyboard for simple word processing
- enjoy the challenge of experimenting with new materials
- enjoy learning mathematical and scientific concepts, such as adding and subtracting numbers
- perform simple calculations in their head
- begin to understand how to tell the time
- may be interested in design and in working models
- enjoy learning about living things and about the world around them
- are able to arrive at logical conclusions and to understand cause and effect.

▲ Drawing a person in detail

See clip 31 on DVD

See clip 32 on DVD

▲ Enjoying learning about living things

Communication and language development

From the age of 7, children:

- begin to understand book language and that stories have characters and a plot (the narrative)
- respond to questions about others in relative terms – for example, 'She is better at running than me'
- like to express and communicate their thoughts – about a book they have read or a TV programme they have seen
- enjoy word games and riddles.

Personal, emotional and social development

From the age of 7, children:

- learn how to control their emotions – they realise that they can keep their own thoughts private and hide their true feelings
- begin to think in terms not only of who they are, but also of who they would like to be
- are completely independent in washing, dressing and toileting skills
- may be able to speak up for themselves, for example, when visiting the dentist or the doctor
- may be critical of their own work at school
- form close friendships, mostly within their own sex.

See clip 33 on DVD

Moral and spiritual development

From the age of 7, children:

- have a clear sense of right and wrong – for example, they realise that it is wrong to hurt other people physically. They are beginning to internalise a sense of justice through co-operation and mutual respect.

- express feelings of awe and wonder, particularly about nature, plants and insects.

Play

From the age of 7, children:

- engage in complex co-operative play, using more people, props and ideas

- take part in games with rules.

ICT guidelines for children aged five to eight years

Using computers

As children increasingly develop language and literacy skills, they are no longer limited to icons and pictures on the screen for understanding. Simple word processors become important educational tools as children experiment with written language. The teacher still needs to monitor what children do, but they are increasingly able to choose and direct their own activities.

Using tape recorders

Using tape recorders promotes early literacy skills: speaking, listening, reading and writing. Apart from following the text in a book while listening to a taped story, children can also record their own made-up stories, poems and songs, or record themselves reading aloud. Adults can then transcribe their stories – or write them down – using the children's own recorded words. In this way, children can see how the spoken word can turn into the written word.

Cameras

Cameras – both still and video – can provide a useful record of children's activities while they are at work, as well as performances and special events. These photos or films can then be added to, with children writing a storyboard or simply providing captions to the photos.

Promoting development

- Encourage vigorous outdoor play – on swings and climbing frames, and in skipping and hopping games such as hopscotch.

- Take children swimming, skating or riding, or to a dancing or martial arts class.

- Arrange an obstacle course for children to navigate bikes around.

- Provide a range of drawing and craft materials, such as charcoal, paint, clay and materials for collage.

- Help children to make a safe den, using a tepee design with sticks and a blanket.

- Encourage children in simple gardening skills, such as digging, planting, raking and watering.

- Promote creative expression in the form of written stories, poetry, dance, drama and making music.

- Take children to see plays and puppet shows.

- Involve children in a puppet show – both in making the puppets and in acting out a play.

- Try some simple cause-and-effect experiments. For example, you could demonstrate how a waterwheel works.

- Try growing some simple crystals.

- Encourage children to plan and make working models, such as cranes, pulley lifts and wheeled vehicles, using recycled materials.

- Introduce children to the customs of different religions, such as Diwali, Ramadan and Christmas.

- Encourage children to become more familiar with using a computer, for instance keying in letters, numbers and punctuation marks.

- Encourage children to share stories together – even a child who is not yet fluent at reading will still enjoy trying to read to a younger child.

- Allow children to run simple errands on their own, for example to post a letter.

Safety points
- Teach children never to put a plastic bag on their head.
- Teach children only ever to buy sweets from a shop and never to accept them from a stranger.

Activities

Numberbo nds

This is a game that can be played by two people. One player calls out a number under ten. The other player answers with the number that brings the total of the two numbers to ten.

This has to be done as quickly as possible: if you hesitate, you are out! For example:

Player 1, 'Six'; Player 2, 'Four'.

Player 1, 'Two'; Player 2, 'Eight'.

Player 1, 'Three'; Player 2, 'Er… er…!'

Player 2 is out!

Take it in turns to go first. Before you start, decide how many times you are going to play the game.

When the child is confident about numbers adding up to ten, you can vary the game by moving up to a larger number. Try twenty. Then go on to one hundred. Children will need a little more time to think as the numbers get bigger.

A sound experiment

Make a yogurt-pot telephone.

You will need:

- two empty, clean yogurt pots
- a ball of string
- scissors.

To make the telephone:

1 Using the scissors, make a small hole in the bottom of each of the pots.

2 Cut a very long piece of string, and push one end through the bottom of each pot.

3 Tie a knot inside each pot to stop the string from coming out.

4 Ask a child to hold one of the pots to his or her ear. Now move away from the child until the string is straight and pulled tight. (You could do this yourself, or give the second pot to another child.)

5 Now send a telephone message to the child by speaking into the pot.

Children will learn that the sound of a voice makes the pot vibrate and that the vibrations pass as sound waves along the string to the other pot and into the other person's ear.

 Observation point

Observe a child during a physical exercise activity. Focus on the child's gross and fine motor skills. You could observe, for example:
- how the child runs, skips or hops
- their sense of balance
- their dexterity when kicking a ball or throwing and catching balls or hoops
- their ability to control a bike and to swerve around an obstacle course.

15 Eight to twelve years

Between the ages of 8 and 12, there may be quite a marked difference in the size and abilities of children. Most girls experience the start of puberty between the ages of 9 and 13; boys first experience puberty between the ages of 10 and 16.

The timing of the onset of puberty will affect the way children get along with others, how they feel about themselves and what they do. Friends become increasingly important, as do having the right clothes and the right look.

Physical development

Children's height and weight continue to increase at a steady rate, and both strength and physical co-ordination skills are also increasing. Typically, children are very energetic and have a large appetite.

Gross motor skills

Children aged 8 and 9 years:

- have increased body strength and co-ordination and a quicker reaction time
- can ride a two-wheel bicycle easily
- can skip freely
- enjoy active, energetic games and sports
- often enjoy participating in competitive sports.

Children aged 10 and 11 years:

- differ in physical maturity; because girls experience puberty earlier they are generally as much as two years ahead of boys
- have body proportions that are becoming similar to those of adults.

Fine motor skills

Children aged 8 and 9 years:

- have more control over small muscles and therefore write and draw with greater skill and dexterity
- draw people with details of clothing and facial features
- draw in a more naturalistic way; techniques of showing depth, shading, three-dimensions and movement begin to develop
- are beginning to join letters together in handwriting – this is called cursive script.

▲ Mastering joined-up writing

Children aged 10 and 11 years:

- tackle more detailed tasks, such as needlework or woodwork

- have an established writing style, usually with joined-up letters.

Cognitive development

Children aged 8 and 9 years:

- have an increased ability to remember and pay attention, and to speak and express their ideas

- are learning to plan ahead and evaluate what they do

- have an increased ability to think and to reason

- can deal with abstract ideas

- enjoy different types of activities – such as joining clubs, playing games with rules and collecting things

- enjoy projects that are task-oriented, such as sewing and woodwork.

Children aged 10 and 11 years:

- begin to understand the motives behind the actions of another

- can concentrate on tasks for increasing periods

- can write fairly lengthy essays

- begin to devise memory strategies

- may be curious about drugs, alcohol and tobacco

- may develop special talents, showing particular skills in writing, maths, art, music or practical pursuits such as woodwork or needlework.

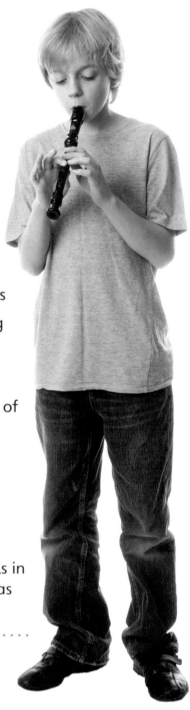

▲ Playing a musical instrument

Communication and language development

Children aged 8 and 9 years:

- use and understand complex sentences
- are highly verbal and enjoy making up and telling jokes
- can read stories with increasing fluency
- use reference books with increasing skill.

Children aged 10 and 11 years:

- use language effectively for a variety of purposes
- use more specific vocabulary and grammar
- understand jokes and riddles based on word ambiguity
- understand most common idioms
- are able to deduce the meanings of unfamiliar words through their knowledge of root words, prefixes and suffixes
- can write for a variety of purposes, using effective vocabulary and varying sentence structure.

Personal, emotional and social development

Children aged 8 and 9 years:

- have a growing sensitivity and begin to realise that others experience feelings of anger, fear and sadness similar to their own
- are easily embarrassed
- become discouraged easily
- take pride in their competence
- can be argumentative and bossy, but equally can be generous and responsive

- are beginning to see things from another's point of view, but still have trouble fully understanding the feelings and needs of other people

- form friendships quite casually and may change them very rapidly; friends are still primarily of the same gender, although they are beginning to show interest in the opposite sex

- like to belong to informal clubs formed by children themselves; also like to belong to more structured adult-led groups, such as Cubs or Brownies

- begin to display a sense of loyalty to a group

- enjoy secrets and jokes.

Children aged 10 and 11 years:

- show an increasing ability to understand the needs and opinions of others

- can identify and label or describe what they are feeling

- become increasingly self-conscious

- usually have a best friend and may form more intense, longer-lasting friendships on the basis of a variety of shared interests and things in common

▶ Friends are still usually of the same gender

- may be experiencing sudden, dramatic, emotional changes associated with puberty (especially girls, who experience puberty earlier than boys)

- have a more defined personality – their idea of self being partly defined by the school environment

- tend to be particularly sensitive to criticism

- prefer to spend leisure time with friends and continue to belong to small groups of the same sex

- are acutely aware of the opposite sex

- succumb to peer pressure more readily and want to talk, dress and act just like friends

- become self-absorbed and introspective

- are more independent, but still like adults to be present to help them.

Moral and spiritual development

Children aged 8 and 9 years:

- continue to think that rules are permanent and unchangeable because they are made up by adults who must be obeyed and respected

- have a clear idea of the difference between reality and fantasy, and are developing their own personal standards of right and wrong

- are highly concerned with fairness.

Children aged 10 and 11 years:

- understand that certain rules can be changed by mutual negotiation and that they are not always imposed by external authority; often, they do not accept rules that they did not help make

- begin to experience conflict between parents' values and those of their peers.

Play

Children need play just as much at this stage of development as they do earlier. By encouraging play both in and away from school, adults can give children the opportunities to interact with their peers and to learn about their environment from first-hand experience.

Children aged 8–11:

- enjoy co-operative and competitive games

- are very active and love being outdoors; physical exercise is vital for developing muscle strength

- enjoy traditional board games, such as draughts and chess, word games, card games and quiz-type games, as well as the more complex fantasy games

- enjoy craft activities and making things from construction kits.

ICT guidelines for children aged eight to twelve years

Safety when using the internet

Adult supervision and advice are essential both at home and at school. Parents need to set boundaries for computer and internet use – for example:

- when and how long they can be online

- which areas of the worldwide web are appropriate to visit (favourite sites can be bookmarked to provide easy access)

- being in the same room when a young child uses the computer, or keeping the computer in an area where other family members are usually present; this will help to promote interaction and technological expertise.

See also page 136 for the importance of e-safety for children and young people.

Promoting development

- Encourage children to take part in physical activities – such as dance, yoga and gymnastics.

- Encourage children to collect things such as shells, stamps or flowers.

- Encourage pretend play, because it still provides an important learning experience.

- Make time for running, hopping, skipping, jumping and climbing.

- Encourage children to dance or skip to music.

- Encourage children to talk about their feelings while working or playing together.

- Provide opportunities for practising life skills, for example cooking, sewing and designing dramatic play props.

- Provide time and space for a child to be alone. Time to read, daydream or do schoolwork uninterrupted will be appreciated.

- Teach basic social rules – how to share and co-operate, not to snatch things or shout at people.

- Find local activities where children have opportunities to make friends outside school such as Cubs, a drama group or swimming lessons.

Safety points

- Children should be taught to play sports in appropriate, safe, supervised areas, with proper equipment and rules – e.g. helmets and knee and elbow pads for cycling and for skateboarding.

- Swimming and water safety lessons can prevent drowning.

- Safety instruction regarding matches, fires, lighters, barbecues, campfires, and cooking on stoves or open fires can prevent major burns.

- Make sure you – or another responsible adult – always know where the child is. Establish clear rules that they must come and tell you or contact you before moving on somewhere else.

- Wearing seat belts remains the most important way of preventing major injury or death on the roads.

Moral and spiritual development

Young people aged 12 to 16 years:

- are able to think beyond themselves more and to understand the perspective of another
- develop their own ideas and values, which often challenge those of their parents
- may deliberately flout rules or keep to them only if there is otherwise a risk of being caught.

Promoting development

- Encourage plenty of physical activity. Exercise will help young people burn off excess energy, strengthen developing muscles and sleep better at night. It may also help them become more comfortable in their changing bodies.

- Encourage them to get enough sleep. The growth hormone is released principally at night during sleep, with short bursts every one to two hours during the deep-sleep phase. Young people who are consistently deprived of sleep during puberty are smaller than they should be.

- Encourage healthy eating habits. During adolescence, young people need to take in more calories to fuel their rapid growth.

- Provide honest answers to questions about sex.

- Never criticise their appearance. Adolescents often spend large amounts of time grooming themselves and obsessing over skin-care products. Acne can be a major concern.

▶ Developing a relationship

- Be understanding of their need for physical space. They may withdraw from physical affection with family members during this period; maintain communication, but respect their need for personal space.

- Create opportunities for them to challenge their thinking skills, using brain-teasers and other puzzles.

- Help them research solutions and learn about the history or background to a problem.

- Encourage reading – for study and for pleasure.

- Allow plenty of time for peer interaction.

- Provide opportunities for leadership skills – for example, helping to teach younger children.

- Encourage them to take an active part in setting rules and boundaries, such as what time they are expected to return home in the evening.

- Listen to their ideas and show respect for them; try to involve them in discussing their behavioural rules and consequences.

▼ Socialising with friends becomes more important

- Provide opportunities for participation in *controlled* risky activities, for example involvement in (properly supervised) sports, such as parachuting or rock climbing.

- Provide opportunities for involvement in community activities, for example volunteering at a homeless shelter or a day centre for disabled people.

- Talk to them about their views and encourage debate. Find out what they think about news stories on television or in the paper; ask them about their political and spiritual beliefs.

- Encourage involvement in projects or activities both within school and after school. At the same time, encourage them to stick with a project or activity long enough to establish some skills.

- Praise them for their efforts as well as their abilities. This will help them to persevere with activities instead of giving up if they are not immediately successful.

- Help them to explore career goals and options. Set up opportunities for them to 'job shadow' others. It is important for them to find out what they *don't* like doing, as well as what they enjoy.

Safety points

- To be safe in sports:
  - take a few minutes to warm up before you play and warm down afterwards
  - know the rules and use them
  - assess the hazards and risks of the sport and know how to control them
  - have the right equipment and use it properly
  - have the right skill level and go to training sessions to improve them.

- When using public transport, keep your fare or pass separate so you don't have to get your purse or wallet out in public.

- Try to stay away from isolated bus stops, especially after dark.

▼ Playing pool together

The importance of e-safety for children and young people

Most young people in this age group have access to the internet and the use of a mobile phone. The internet has become an everyday tool in family life, whether accessed from a computer or a mobile phone. It is used for online banking, buying and selling goods, finding information and for socialising with others. However, the internet also has a darker side, with cyber crime, inappropriate material and illegal activity taking place online, affecting adults, children and young people. As it is not realistic (or desirable) to forbid use of the internet, education about using the internet safely is essential.

What are the risks?

Cyberbullying

This is when one person or a group of people try to threaten, tease or embarrass someone else by using a mobile phone or the internet. Text messages, prank mobile phone calls and content posted on social networking sites are all examples of the growing threat of cyberbullying.

Online grooming

Child sex abusers find the internet a convenient place to participate in a range of child sexual abuse activity – including contact with children and young people – as they can remain anonymous. They feel a sense of security by operating from the safety of their own homes and have also been known to set up fake email accounts and chat personas to mask their real identity online.

Young people often feel more confident when chatting on the internet than they do in other situations, and can be tempted to say and do things that they would not even consider if they were meeting someone face to face. The consequences of this freedom include the young person:

- becoming drawn into repeated contact and intimacy online with a stranger; IM (Instant Messaging) is a more intimate area than a chat room and the young person may feel a sense of trust because a 'friend-of-a-friend' knows them

◉ giving out personal information such as mobile numbers and pictures of themselves

◉ being groomed when this information is misused; other sex-abusers may respond when the young person's image is posted on a website.

ICT guidelines for children and young people

Although the risk of encountering a child sexual offender online is thought to be small, all children and young people should be taught the safety lessons of using the internet. The following guidelines apply to anyone who uses the internet to chat online.

- Use child protection services – find out what child protection services your Internet Service Provider (ISP) offers. Most ISPs provide free software to help in child protection.

- Use special internet filtering software – use walled gardens and a child or family-friendly search engine (such as the CBBC Safe Search) with younger children to bookmark favourite sites for children to use.

- Supervise viewing – families should keep their computer in a communal area of the house, where viewing of internet sites can be supervised.

- Keep personal information safe – by never giving it out to strangers. Also never give away friends' details online – their street addresses, email addresses, mobile numbers or anything that could identify them offline. Keep any internet passwords secret too.

- Never meet up with someone you have only met in a chat room, no matter how long you've known them and how tempting it seems.

- Filter emails – watch out for emails from people unknown to you. Never accept these or open any attachments.

- Be wary of lies – it's easy to lie online. People may not be who they say they are: child sex offenders often pretend to be the same age as the child or a little older.

- Check chat rooms – children and young people love to chat but make sure they only use moderated chat rooms; most have an alert button you can press if you feel concerned about another chatter's behaviour or you could keep a record of worrying conversations by hitting 'print screen'. Encourage children to tell you if they feel uncomfortable, upset or threatened by anything they see online. Never say anything in a chat room that you wouldn't say in public. Remember, you are in control and can leave a chat room or log off at any time.

- Get advice – all schools should have an e-Safety Policy and an e-Safety Co-ordinator who will be able to advise you where to look for more support.

Health education

Many health education topics are now addressed in secondary schools, but there is still a real problem with teenage pregnancies, sexually transmitted diseases (STDs) and alcohol abuse. Adolescents need clear, non-judgemental information about:

- making safe decisions about relationships, sexual intercourse and how to stand up for their decisions
- resisting pressures from friends or others for unwanted sex or drugs
- how to recognise and avoid or leave a situation that may be risky or turn violent
- finding out where friendly local youth services are and how to access them
- how to ensure they have safer sex
- the risks to health and safety from drinking too much alcohol.

17 Developmental assessment

This section looks briefly at the standard developmental assessments carried out under the NHS in the UK on children from birth to the age of 5. After the age of 5, the school health service takes over the assessments.

If a child has a developmental delay, carers will want to know about the problem as soon as possible: it is often easier to come to terms with a serious problem in a young baby than in an older child.

Health professionals should always take carers' concerns seriously and must never treat parents or other carers as fussy, neurotic or over-anxious.

The Healthy Child Programme

The Healthy Child Programme is a series of reviews, screening tests, vaccinations and information that supports parents and helps them to give their child the best chance of staying healthy and well. The Healthy Child team is led by a health visitor, who works closely with the GP. The team includes people with different skills and experience, such as nursery nurses, children's nurses and Early Years support staff.

The Personal Child Health Record (PCHR)

Shortly before or after a baby is born, parents are given a Personal Child Health Record (PCHR). In most areas of England and in Scotland, this has a red cover and is often called the red book. This is a way of keeping track of the child's progress and can be added to by parents – for example, to record any accidents, illnesses or details of medicines prescribed.

Records are kept of the child's:

- height and weight
- immunisations
- childhood illnesses and accidents.

Development reviews

Regular development reviews are carried out in child health clinics and at the child's home by general practitioners, health visitors and school nurses. If the child's first language is not English, development reviews can be carried out with the help of someone who can speak the child's language.

Children's holistic development is reviewed as:

- gross motor skills: sitting, standing, walking, running
- fine motor skills: handling toys, stacking bricks, doing up buttons and tying shoelaces (gross and fine manipulative skills)
- speech and language, including hearing
- vision
- social behaviour.

Reviews give parents and carers opportunities to say what they have noticed about their child. They can also discuss anything that concerns them about their child's health and behaviour.

Ages for reviews

Note that in some parts of the country, especially after the age of 3, the ages at which children are reviewed may vary slightly from those given below.

Assessment of the newborn baby

Shortly after birth, the newborn baby is examined by a paediatrician or family doctor. Specific checks are made to assess the development of the baby:

- the baby is weighed
- the spine is checked for any evidence of spina bifida
- the mouth is checked for evidence of a cleft palate —a gap in the roof of the mouth
- the head is checked for size and shape, and the head circumference is measured
- the eyes are checked for cataracts
- the neck is examined for any obvious injury to the neck muscles after a difficult birth

- the hands are checked for webbing (fingers joined together at the base) or creases (a single unbroken crease from one side of the palm to the other is one feature of Down's syndrome)
- the hips are tested for congenital dislocation
- the feet are checked for webbing and talipes (club foot)
- the reflex actions are observed (see pages 8 and 12–13)
- the hearing is tested, often by means of Otoacoustic Emissions Testing(OAE) or the cradle test: this involves placing a sponge earphone into the ear canal, then stimulating the ear with sound and measuring an echo – the echo is found in all normal-hearing individuals, so its absence may indicate a hearing loss and the need for further testing.

Other medical checks include:

- listening to the heart and lungs to detect any abnormality
- examining the anus and the genitalia for any malformation.

▲ A newborn baby

Assessment by 14 days

A health professional, usually a health visitor, will carry out a new baby review. Advice is also given on feeding the baby, becoming a parent and how to help the baby grow up healthily. The baby should be weighed (naked) at birth and at five and ten days old.

Assessment at 4–5 years

Discussion

Carers are asked if they have any general concerns about the child's development or about emotional or behavioural problems.

The doctor will also be concerned with the child's ability to concentrate, to play with others and to separate from the main carer without distress.

Observation

Motor skills are checked:

- can the child walk, run and climb stairs
- does the child tire more quickly than other children?

Fine manipulative skills are checked:

- can the child control pencils and paint brushes
- can the child draw a cross?

▲ Hopping, demonstrating motor skills

◀ Drawing a cross, demonstrating fine manipulative skills

Vision, language and hearing are also assessed, by observation and by discussion with the carers. If there are any particular problems, specialist assessment can be arranged.

Measurement

Height and weight are measured and plotted on the growth chart.

Examination

Other checks will depend on any concerns that the carer or the doctor may have. For example, if the child has asthma an examination of the lungs may take place.

The school health team continues to monitor the health and development of all schoolchildren up to the age of 16. Teachers and other education professionals may refer any pupil for assessment, and school nurses are increasingly involved in health education programmes within schools.

18 Children with additional needs

The term additional needs is used to describe children whose development differs from the norm.

Like that of all other children, the development of children with additional needs is influenced by:

- the quality of their experiences
- the quality of their social relationships
- the learning opportunities they are offered.

Sometimes the additional need is identified before birth or soon after. Other additional needs, such as a heart disorder or a visual or hearing impairment, may become apparent only much later.

What are additional needs?

Children with additional needs are not an easily defined group. Some have a very obvious and well-researched disability, such as Down's syndrome or cerebral palsy; others may have a specific learning difficulty such as dyslexia. What defines them as children with additional needs is the fact that they need *additional help* in some areas of development when compared with other children.

It is important to remember that children are more alike than different. Children with disabilities share the same basic needs as other children, but the disabilities may affect the meeting of those needs or create additional needs. Thus a child who lacks speech may find it difficult to communicate needs or make friends and a child who lacks mobility may be isolated by not being able to join in the activities of others. Children need to feel welcome and they need to feel safe, both physically and emotionally. They also need to have friends and to feel that they belong. All children should be encouraged to live up to their potential, and every child should be celebrated for his or her uniqueness. Always look at children as individuals first, and *then* consider their additional needs.

▼ Encouraging participation in a group activity

Kinds of additional need

Additional needs may be grouped into the following categories:

- *physical impairment* – needs related to problems with mobility or co-ordination, and sometimes dyspraxia

- *sensory impairment* – needs related to problems with sight or hearing

- *speech or language difficulties* – needs related to problems such as delayed language, difficulties in articulation or stuttering

- *moderate to severe learning disabilitie*s – needs related to problems many of which result from a genetic defect or from an accident or a trauma

- *specific learning difficulties (SLD)* – needs related to problems with the areas of reading, writing or numeracy (usually)

- *a medical condition* – needs related to conditions such as asthma, cystic fibrosis or diabetes

- *emotional difficulties* – needs related to conditions such as anxiety, fear, depression, autism or autistic spectrum disorder

- *behavioural difficulties* – needs related to aggression, attention deficit hyperactivity disorder(ADHD),or antisocial behaviour

- *giftedness* – needs related to being highly gifted, academically or artistically.

Short-termneeds

Some children may have an additional need at a particular time only, such as when a parent or sibling has died, or when they have been a victim of bullying or abuse.

Inclusive care and education

Children have special educational needs (SEN) if they have a learning difficulty that calls for extra support. A child may also develop special needs as the result of an accident or illness – for example, meningitis can cause sensory impairments.

A learning difficulty means that the child finds it more difficult to learn than most other children of the same age, or has a disability that makes it difficult for her or him to use ordinary school facilities. One in five children may have special educational needs at some stage during their education. These may be apparent at a very early age or may develop later.

The Children Act 2004 promotes the integration of disabled children in mainstream settings, such as nursery schools, day nurseries, schools and children's centres. This approach is called inclusive care and educationa nd recognises that care and education are inextricably linked.

Providing for children with additional needs

Child development centres

In some areas, teams of professionals – doctors, therapists, health visitors and social workers – are available to help support children with additional needs and their families. Usually such teams work from a child development centre. Parents can be referred to this service by their general practitioner or health visitor.

Specialisthelp

Many services are available to help children who have additional needs to learn and develop. For example:

- physiotherapy
- speech and language therapy
- occupational therapy
- home learning schemes – such as the Portages cheme, which provides trained home visitors to work with parents and their young children
- equipment and special aids provisions, such as pushchairs, wheelchairs, communication aids or hearing aids

- financial support for families where children need help with personal care and/or mobility

- toy libraries – most areas have a toy library for children with additional needs from which specially chosen toys can be borrowed for use at home

- specialist playgroups, opportunity groups and children's centres – these centres often provide on-site physiotherapy, nursing care and play therapy

- respite care – for instance, Crossroads, a national voluntary organisation that provides trained care assistants for the practical respite care needed by some children with disabilities

- playgroups – state-run, privately run or voluntary

- nurseries, school nurseries and classes.

To find out what's available in your area, ask your health visitor, your GP, the social services department or the educational adviser for additional needs at your local education department.

▼ Promoting the development of motor skills and co-ordination

Promoting development in children with additional needs

Many children with additional needs who attend mainstream nurseries and schools will require one-to-one attention from a trained early years worker. The following sections provide some ideas for those working with children with additional needs.

Children with physical impairments

Children with physical limitations have specific needs depending on their particular disability.

Friends and classmates are usually eager to assist a child with a physical difficulty. Although such helpful behaviour should be applauded, children with physical problems also need encouragement to do as much as possible for themselves. This may mean that tasks and chores take a little more time, but being patient and encouraging promotes self-confidence and independence.

Difficulties

Children who have difficulties with gross motor skills:
- may stumble and trip frequently
- may have difficulty walking or running, jumping or climbing, or be unable to do these at all
- may have poor balance
- may have difficulty in bouncing, catching or throwing balls
- may be unable to release objects voluntarily.

Children who have difficulties with fine motor skills:
- may have poorly developed hand or finger co-ordination
- may have difficulty in picking up small objects
- may have difficulty in drawing or writing.

Children with hearing impairment

Children who have difficulty hearing need opportunities to learn how to listen and speak. Provide activities that encourage communication and language development. Children can develop important language skills with practice. Activities with very little verbal interaction are also very important.

Difficulties

Children with hearing impairment:

- may not respond when spoken to
- may not startle at a loud noise
- may not wake up in response to sound
- may talk but be impossible to understand
- may leave out many sounds when talking
- may seem unable to follow verbal directions
- may hold their head so that one ear is turned toward the speaker
- may talk in a very loud or a very soft voice
- may coo or gurgle, but may not progress to saying words
- may talk very little or not at all
- may talk in a monotone voice
- may interrupt conversations or seem unaware that others are talking
- may be alert and attentive to things that can be seen, but not to those others would hear.

Promotingd evelopment

Make sure that the environment is suitable:

- During activities, cut down on background noise from the radio and machines, such as dishwashers. Use carpets, rugs and pillows to absorb excess sound.

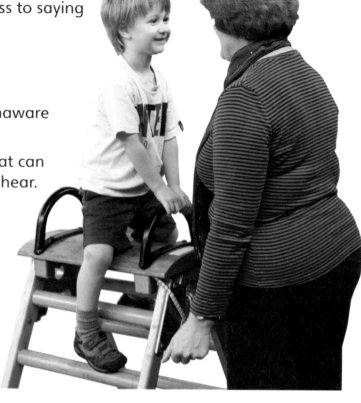
▼ Enjoying a sense of achievement

- Provide children with visual cues. For example, label shelves with a picture of toys to make tidying away toys easier. Use pictures to illustrate the steps of a recipe during cooking activities.

- Make eye contact before you start to speak. A gentle tap on the shoulder will usually get a child's attention.

- Talk in a normal voice – do not shout. Use gestures and facial expressions to clarify your message.

Provide suitable equipment:

- Provide headphones, or set up a special area where a tape recorder can be played at a higher volume.

- Provide toys that make a lot of noise – children can feel the vibrations even when they cannot hear the sound.

- Find out how to look after hearing aids and how to protect them from loss or damage within the school or nursery – for example, sand and dirt can damage them.

Offer appropriate activities:

- Teach children to use gestures and sign language, for example Signalong, Makaton or the Picture Exchange Communication System (PECS).

- Encourage children to talk about what they are doing. Ask open-ended questions that require an answer; these will encourage the child to practise using language.

- Use stories, songs and finger-play to enhance language development.

- Repeat favourite rhymes and songs to encourage confidence in developing language skills.

- Encourage dancing to music: children will feel the vibrations and enjoy the chance to express themselves.

Children with learning disabilities

Children with learning disabilities will usually go through the typical sequence of developmental stages, but at a much slower rate. Characteristics vary widely with different disabilities, but a few approaches can be applied to all.

Difficulties

Children with learning difficulties:

- may have a short attention span and be easily distracted
- may have difficulty in making transitions, such as from one class to the next
- may prefer to play with younger children
- may speak and use language like a much younger child
- may be afraid of trying new things
- may have difficulty in problem-solving
- may not remember things well
- may not be able to transfer learning to a new situation
- may repeat the same movement over and over again.

▼ Playing with other children promotes emotional and social development

Make sure that the environment is suitable:

- Keep verbal instructions simple.

- Tell children how to do something and show them by guiding their hands and body through the movements of an activity.

- Avoid sudden transitions. When it's time to end an activity or to move to another activity, give the child plenty of warning.

- Provide cues to help children know what is expected from them – for example, mark their coat hook with a picture of a child hanging up a coat.

- Expect appropriate behaviour – don't allow a child with a learning disability to behave in ways that are not allowed in other children.

- Provide opportunities to play near a child who is doing a similar activity. This can give the child with learning difficulties some ideas about how to use and explore the same materials.

Offer appropriate activities:

- Break activities into small steps and give one instruction at a time.

- Practise activities over and over again.

- Allow children plenty of time to practise new things that they are learning.

- Select activities that match the child's mental age and abilities.

- Try not to overwhelm the child with too many toys or art materials at once.

Provide suitable equipment:

- Make sure that there are obvious differences in size, shape and colour when sorting or classifying objects. Differences that are too subtle, such as between maroon and red, or oval shapes and circles, may be confusing.

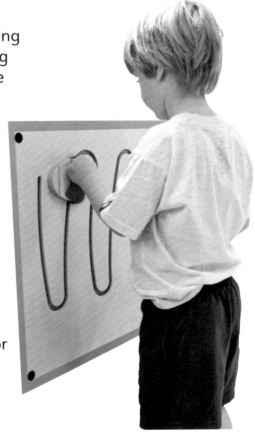

▲ Using interactive games to promote hand-eye co-ordination

Children with behavioural difficulties

Children with behavioural difficulties often display one of three types of extreme behaviour: withdrawal, aggression or hyperactivity. Each type of behaviour may require a different strategy to promote social and emotional development.

Difficulties

Children with behavioural difficulties:

- may use aggressive behaviour to deal with most situations
- may show extreme fear and anxiety
- may seem not to recognise basic feelings of happiness, sadness, anger or fear
- may always react in the same way, such as crying or hitting
- may not want to be touched
- may withdraw or stay quiet and passive most of the time
- may show excessive activity, restlessness or inability to stick to a task
- may regress to babyish behaviour whenever stress occurs
- may cry a great deal, seem depressed and unhappy, and seldom laugh.

▼ A soft playroom provides a safe area for physical exercise and play

Promotingd evelopment

Make sure that the environment is suitable:

- Treat children uniquely. Always take them seriously, and show that you believe in them.
- Listen to each child with respect. Don't compare the child who is being aggressive with another child who is playing well.
- Invite a withdrawn child to join in an activity by watching others. As the child becomes more comfortable, demonstrate how to play with materials or toys. Encourage the child to play along with you.

- Watch for signs of aggressive behaviour and intervene quickly. Teach problem-solving skills.

Offer appropriate activities:

- Provide developmentally appropriate activities that are not overly difficult and which will help the child feel capable. Avoid activities that can be done in only one way.

- Watch for periods when children are less excitable and more in control. Use these times to present a new activity that requires some concentration.

- Keep stories and group activities short to match attention spans. Seat the child near you and away from distractions such as a nearby shelf of toys.

- Avoid over-stimulation. Limit the number of toys or materials you set out at one time.

- Provide adult guidance and structure. Help children to plan or to organise an activity. For example, if a child wants to play at being a firefighter you could suggest some props, such as a bucket and a blanket, and perhaps invite other children to play.

- Announce the tidying-up time and other transitions ahead of time. During the transition, give the child a specific task.

◀ Promoting skills of independence

Children with autism (autistic spectrum disorder – ASD)

Autism is a disability that disrupts the development of social interaction and communication. Children are affected in many different ways by autism, which is why we use the term autistic spectrum. The most seriously affected children have profound learning disabilities and delayed language, and will need intensive support and care. At the other end of the autistic spectrum, children with Asperger's syndrome may cope with the intellectual demands of schooling very well, although they will still find aspects of social interaction and communication difficult. The onset of autism is almost always before the age of 3 years. It affects four times as many boys as girls.

Difficulties

Children with autism:

- may find it difficult to interact socially – not understanding social rules, behaviour and relationships – for example, appearing indifferent to other people or not understanding how to take turns

- may find social communication difficult – for example, not fully understanding the meaning of common gestures, facial expressions or tone of voice

- may show rigidity of thinking and difficulties with social imagination – for example, having a limited range of imaginative activities, possibly copied and pursued rigidly and repetitively

- may show resistance to any change in routine.

Promotingd evelopment

- Putting things into symbols can help, as visual learning is stronger than language-based learning

- Provide a visual timetable, showing the main sequence of events and routines in the day. This can help the child to understand what is going to happen next.

- Promote early communication by using symbols that the child can pick up or point to, in order to make choices and express preferences.

- Reduce visual stimulation by keeping displays and labels orderly: pictures all over the windows and labels at jaunty angles can be visually overwhelming. Have some places with blank walls, which can be calming.

- Keep everything as clear and consistent as you can – for many children with an ASD sudden changes in routine can be very scary.

- Alert the child when something is about to happen by using symbols or the visual timetable. When something new is coming up, try to prepare the child as much as you can. You might have a symbol that means 'a change' or be able to use a photograph to signal what is going to happen.

- Use as few words and as few symbols as possible: communicate clearly and briefly.

- Show how things work by demonstrating step by step – for example, when putting Lego® bricks together.

- Allow plenty of time and encourage the child to copy you.

- Introduce new things slowly – for example, start a sand play activity in a quiet area without any other children and encourage the child to touch a small amount of sand on a tabletop or on the floor.

Children with attention deficit hyperactivity disorder (ADHD)

ADHD is a specific learning difficulty, which usually starts at about 18 months but might not be diagnosed until later (even until adulthood). It is estimated that ADHD affects five to ten per cent of children and adolescents in the UK, with up to one in 100 severely affected. Symptoms usually become apparent between the ages of three and seven, with boys more likely to be affected than girls. The condition can run in families. Children with ADHD have problems with focusing their attention and, at the same time, are hyperactive.

Difficulties

Children with ADHD:

- may have difficulty remaining seated when asked to do so
- find it difficult to share and take turns in group situations
- may talk excessively
- may be easily distracted by extraneous stimuli
- appear not to be listening when being spoken to
- appear restless, often fidgeting with hands or feet
- have difficulty playing quietly
- may often lose things necessary for tasks or activities at school or at home – for example, books and pencils
- have difficulty sustaining attention in tasks or play activities
- may constantly interrupt others – for example, pushing into other children's games
- may have low self-esteem
- often engage in physically dangerous activities without considering possible consequences – for example, running across the road without looking
- may be unable to focus attention on relevant detail at an age when such control is expected.

Promotingd evelopment

Treatment may be by a stimulant medication (usually Ritalin®) which often has an immediate improving effect on the child's behaviour, but is a controversial treatment. Arriving at the correct dosage for the individual takes time and a high degree of co-operation between the parents and other professionals. It is generally agreed that medical treatment on its own is not an appropriate response to ADHD, and should be combined with the following management techniques:

- therapeutic input – for example, art therapy, occupational therapy or counselling for older children

- a programme to help with managing behaviour – setting clear limits, helping children anticipate difficulties and find their own ways of coping – for example, taking a moment or two out, or engaging in something calming

- lifestyle changes – for example, watching less television, spending less time on computers and electronic games, taking more exercise, and eating more healthily

- helping children to become more organised – use diaries, notebooks, lists, notes to parents or carers, reminders about equipment etc.

- making a timetable – set specific times for waking up, eating, playing, doing homework, doing chores, watching TV or playing video games, and going to bed. Put the timetable where the child will always see it. Explain any changes to the routine in advance.

- encouraging children to look at you when you are talking to them and maintain eye contact – repeat instructions and ask them to say the instructions back to you

- ensuring that children are supervised all the time – because they are impulsive, children who have ADHD may need more adult supervision than other children their age

- choosing a regular place for doing homework – away from distractions such as other people, TV and video games. Break homework time into small parts allow for short breaks between activities.

- repeating rules frequently – 'dos' will work better than 'don'ts'

- praising and rewarding each effort and appropriate behaviour

- avoiding confrontations where possible and staying calm

- alerting children when changing activities in the classroom – for example, 'In five minutes, we will be going into the hall for PE'.

Assessment of children with additional needs

Local education authorities that think a child over 2 years old may have special educational needs must make an assessment of their needs. For children under 2, an assessment must be made if parents ask for it.

This assessment is a way of getting advice about the child's educational needs, and parents can take part in the assessment. The Advisory Centre for Education (see page 204) offers advice and produces a handbook on the subject.

▲ Helping a child to focus in a structured activity session

Voluntary organisations

There are many voluntary organisations that focus on particular disabilities and illnesses; these organisations are a valuable source of information, advice and support for parents and professionals. Through them, parents can often be put in touch with other parents in similar situations. Contact a Family (see page 204) is the national voluntary organisation that provides mutual support and advice for groups of families living in the same neighbourhood whose children have additional needs.

Children with additional needs – a checklist

The following questions can help parents and carers to ensure that they receive the help and support they need.

1 Is there a name for my child's condition? If so, what is it?

2 Are more tests needed to get a clear diagnosis or to confirm what has been found out?

3 Is the condition likely to get worse, or will it stay roughly the same?

4 Where is the best place to go for medical help?

5 Where is the best place to go for practical help?

6 How can I get in touch with other parents who have children with a similar condition?

7 How can I find out how best to help my child?

19 Theories of child development

Most theories of child development rely to a great extent on the detailed observation of children in their own cultural contexts.

Studying the way in which children think, learn, behave and feel helps to advance our understanding of child development.

Recent advances in neuroscience have also increased our knowledge about the ways in which children develop and learn.

Neuroscience

Current research into the development and learning of babies and young children focuses on neuroscience. Neuroscience is the study of all aspects of the brain and the nervous system, in health and in disease. In the past, some scientists thought that the brain's development was determined genetically and that brain growth followed a biologically predetermined path. It was also thought, until fairly recently, that the human brain stopped developing after early childhood and remained fixed for the rest of our lives. However, new research is showing that our brains continue to develop well into our teens and even early twenties – particularly the area of the brain involved in social interaction and decision-making.

How the brain works

It is estimated that at birth, a baby's brain contains thousands of millions of neurons or nerve cells, and that almost all the neurons that the brain will ever have are present. Babies start to learn in the womb, particularly in the last three months. When they are born, babies are able to recognise familiar sounds and they have already developed some taste preferences. The brain continues to grow for a few years after birth and by the age of 2 years, the brain is about 80 per cent of the adult size.

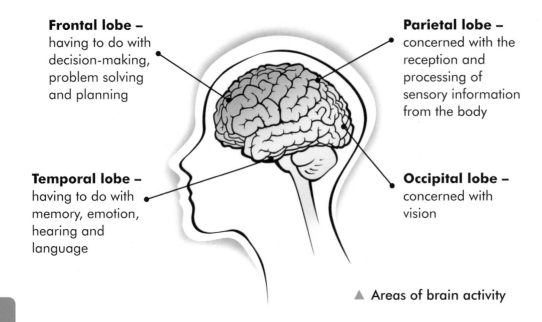

Frontal lobe – having to do with decision-making, problem solving and planning

Parietal lobe – concerned with the reception and processing of sensory information from the body

Temporal lobe – having to do with memory, emotion, hearing and language

Occipital lobe – concerned with vision

▲ Areas of brain activity

Neurons are connected together to form even more billions of different neural pathways. Whenever we have a new experience, a new neural pathway in the brain is used. Each new experience changes our behaviour – this is called learning. If the experience is repeated, or the stimulus is very strong, more nerve impulses are sent along the new pathway. This reinforces the learning process and explains why repetition helps us to learn new things.

Repetition strengthens the connections between neurons and makes it easier for impulses to travel along the pathway. This process is commonly known as hard-wiring and 90 per cent of the hard-wired connections will be complete by the age of three. Hard-wiring is very important to our understanding of brain development in early childhood and explains and illustrates the long-lasting impact of early experiences.

Brain development and the importance of play

Neuroscientists believe that most of the brain's cells are formed before birth, but that most of the connections among cells are made during infancy and early childhood. They refer to the plasticity of the brain and believe that:

⊚ early experiences are vital to healthy brain development. A baby's mind is primed – or ready – for learning but it needs early experiences in order to 'wire' the neural circuits of the brain that facilitate learning.

⊚ the outside world shapes the development of a baby's brain through experiences that a child's senses – vision, hearing, smell, touch and taste – take in.

Play is particularly important to healthy brain development as it allows children to use their creativity while developing their imagination, in addition to their physical, cognitive and emotional skills. It is through play that children at a very early age engage and interact in the world around them.

The following pages summarise the main theories of child development. The main theorists in each area of development are listed in the table.

Cognitive development
Jean Piaget (1896–1980)
Lev Vygotsky (1896–1934)
Jerome Bruner (b. 1915)
Emotional and social development
Sigmund Freud (1856–1939)
E.H. Erikson (1902–1979)
John Bowlby (1907–1990)

Piaget, Bruner and Vygotsky all emphasised cognitive development as being closely linked to the brain's construction of knowledge within a social context.

- **Piaget** considered the most critical factor in a child's cognitive development to be interaction with peers; such interaction provides opportunities for the child to have cognitive conflict, which results in arguing or debating with peers. It also requires children to decentre or consider another person's point of view. Piaget observed that children are most challenged in their thinking when they are with peers because they all are on an equal footing and are freer to confront ideas than when interacting with adults.

- **Bruner** also observed that the process of constructing knowledge of the world is not done in isolation but rather within a social context. The child is a social being and, through social life, acquires a framework for interpreting experiences.

- **Vygotsky** believed that the most fruitful experience in a child's education is their collaboration with more skilled partners. He asserted that the more experienced partner provides help in the way of an intellectual scaffold, which allows the less experienced learner to accomplish more complex tasks than may be possible alone.

Freud, Erikson and Bowlby believed in the importance of detailed observations of children and of gaining close relationships with them.

- **Freud** constructed a stage theory of psychosexual development in children, whom he said were particularly sensitised at certain ages. He also warned that a person could become fixated at a particular stage if their needs were not met.

- **Erikson** accepted Freud's stage theory but also proposed that psychosocial crises beset individuals in adjusting to a particular social environment. His ideas influenced thinking about the development of self-esteem and the self-concept.

- **Bowlby** developed the attachment theory based on his observations of the grief and despair of young children separated for long periods of time from the adult to whom they had become attached (usually their mothers). He concluded that attachment is vital to infants.

Piaget's theory of cognitive development

Piaget believed that there are four major developmental stages between birth and adulthood, through which all children pass in the same sequence, as seen in the flow chart. The ages given are all approximate.

The sensori-motor stage: from birth to 2 years

Babies learn about themselves and their environment through their senses and through their own activity and movements.

- Schemas: babies are developing their first schemas. Schemas are patterns of action that the baby can generalise, and which become increasingly coordinated. For example, at 4½ months the baby can:

  - see a rattle
  - reach out for the rattle
  - grasp the rattle
  - put the rattle in their mouth.

These four schemas are tracking, reaching, grasping and sucking schemas.

- **Centration**: toddlers still see things mainly from their own point of view and cannot decentre to look at things from somebody else's point of view. Furthermore, they tend at any one time to focus on only one aspect of an event – this is known as centration. Piaget describes them as **intellectually egocentric**.

- **People and object permanence**: by the end of their first year, most children have understood that people and objects are permanent and constant, that is, they go on existing even when they cannot be seen (for example if they are under a cloth or in another room).

---

sensori-motor stage
(from birth to 2 years)

pre-operational stage
(from 2 to 7 years)

concrete operations
(from 7 to 12 years)

formal operations
(12 years to adulthood)

Piaget also described six sub-stages in the sensori-motor development stage:

1 *Stage of reflex activity (birth to 1 month)*: grasping, sucking, eye movements, orientation to sound, etc. For example, sucking to obtain milk; pressure on roof of mouth stimulates further sucking and so on.

2 *Stage of primary circular reactions (1 to 4 months)*: the baby's behaviour, by chance, leads to an interesting result and is repeated (*primary* = centre on infant's own body; *circular* = repetition). For example, thumb-sucking.

3 *Stage of secondary circular reactions (4 to 8 months)*: repetition of simple actions on external objects. For example, bangs a toy to make a noise.

▲ Hiding an object...

4 *Co-ordination of secondary circular reactions (8 to 12 months)*: combine actions to achieve a desired effect. The baby learns that it is separate from their environment, and that aspects of their environment – their parents or favourite toy – continue to exist even though they may be outside the reach of their senses. This is called object permanence. For example, knocks a cushion away to reach for a desired toy.

5 *Stage of tertiary circular reactions (12 to 18 months)*: involves the discovery of new methods to meet goals: trial and error. Piaget describes the infant at this stage as the 'young scientist' – making early experiments. For example, an object hidden under one of several covers can be found.

▲ ...looking for it

6 *Beginnings of symbolic representation (18 to 24 months)*: marks the beginnings of insight or true creativity. The infant thinks about a problem before acting and thoughts begin to dominate actions. This marks the passage into unique thought in the later three areas of development. For example, baby searches for a hidden object, certain that it exists somewhere (the final stage of object permanence).

▶ ...and 'finding' it again

Pre-operational stage: from 2 to 7 years

Piaget described the radical change that takes place in children's thinking at around the age of 18 months in terms of the child's ability to use symbols, but he tended to focus on what the child still cannot do rather than on what the child can do.

- *Action schemas* – for example, rotation or trajectory (up and down) – now become representational. Th is means that children begin to use symbolic behaviour, which includes language, representational drawings and pretend play. Action schemas are internalised by the child and they become thinking beings. Thinking backwards and forwards with ideas (concepts) is still strongly linked, however, with perception of immediate experiences (i.e. the perception of objects, people and events).

- *The development of memory* – recalling past perceptions and prior experiences is now important. In their minds, children will form images of a smell, of something they have seen, of something they have heard, of something that moved, of something they tasted or something they touched. They also now anticipate the future.

- *Developing concepts* – they imitate things they remember from past experiences. Using past and future, as well as immediate, experiences, children now begin to develop ideas (concepts). This frees them to think more about time and space.

- *Seriation* – because children still only look at one aspect of a situation, it influences the way that they classify or seriate things (see pages 180–181).

- At this stage, children also tend to assume that objects have consciousness (animism), for example, they get cross with a door for slamming shut, maybe saying 'naughty door'. They also form an idea of what is right or wrong in what actually happens (moral realism).

An example of moral realism

If a cup breaks, children think the person who broke it has been naughty. They are not, at this stage, interested in how the event came about (i.e. the motive). They are likely to think that a child who breaks a cup helping to wash up is naughtier than the child who takes a valuable cup from the shelf when they had been told not to, even if they did not break it.

Concrete operational stage: about 7 to 12 years

Children continue to learn through their experiences with real objects and become capable of logical thought.

- Children now begin to understand class inclusion.

- They begin to understand about the conservation of mass, number, area, quantity, volume and weight. Piaget did not believe it possible to teach conservation, and researchers disagreeing with his point of view have not managed to prove conclusively that it is possible.

- Children realise that things are not always as they look.

- However, they still need *real situations* to help them to think conceptually, and they have great difficulty thinking in the abstract. For example, they need practical work in understanding number or time concepts in mathematics.

- Although children can now see things from somebody else's point of view (this means they have established Theory of Mind), they still tend to try to make ideas fit other ways of thinking.

- They will use *symbols* in writing, reading, notation in music, drawing, maths and dance if they are introduced to these.

- Children at this stage of development can also take into account several features of an object at the same time when they are classifying and seriating. This means that they no longer *centrate*, that is, they no longer concentrate on just one thing at a time. They realise that there might be several correct solutions to a problem or several outcomes of an event or action.

- Children also now enjoy games and understand about *rules in games*, such as football or snakes and ladders.

Conservation

Conservation of thinking means the child can hold in mind several things at once, and can think beyond how something looks. Two beakers might look as if the tall one holds more water than the wider one, but that is only because the height deceives the onlooker. The child needs to realise that width is as important as height in deciding which beaker holds the most water. A child under 5 years old will rarely conserve (that is, the child will assume that the taller glass holds more water).

Piaget's experiments looked at areas such as conservation of shape, weight, volume, speed, number and moral development.

▲ This 7-year old child is 'at' Piaget's concrete operational stage. He understands the concept of reversibility and correctly states that the amount of liquid in the taller glass is exactly the same as in the shorter glass.

Conservation of mass

1 Give children two balls of clay or play dough.
2 Check that the child agrees that there is the same amount in each ball.
3 Roll one into a sausage shape while the child is watching.
4 Then ask if there is the same amount of clay in both pieces as before.

Children under 7 years usually do not conserve mass in a formal test situation like this. This means that they all think that either the sausage shape or the ball shape has more clay in it. This is because these children cannot hold in mind several ideas at once (the balls were the same) but can only concentrate on one aspect (the sausage versus the ball).

▲ This 5-year-old child is 'at' Piaget's preoperational stage. She states that the longer row contains more objects. She is not yet able to 'conserve' number.

Class inclusion

As children develop they gradually begin to link their previous experiences together much more easily: the experiences become more like a video film than a sequence of still photographs. As well as the operational concepts outlined above, children also form concepts about the shapes, sizes, colours and classes of objects and animals. The class of animals might be divided into pets and farm animals, while the class of cutlery might be divided into knives, forks and spoons. This is called class inclusion.

Seriation

During Piaget's concrete operations stage – aged 7 to 12 years – children show increased use of logic or reasoning. They develop the ability to seriate: that is, to sort objects or situations according to any characteristic, such as size, colour, shape or type. Piaget believes that the processes of seriation and of conservation are essential factors for many of the complex types of scientific reasoning including the understanding of number.

Concrete operations and conservation

As concept formation elaborates, children begin to understand that things are not always as they seem to be. This typically occurs as children (aged 7–12 years) begin to go to junior school, according to Piaget. Children can now hold in mind several things at once when they are thinking and they can run backwards and forwards through their thoughts. Piaget says the child's thinking gradually becomes more mobile. Children's concepts develop to include concrete operations, such as the conservation of mass and number.

Formal operational stage: from 12 years to adult

The main features of this stage are:

- *Abstract concepts*: young people begin to develop a more abstract view of the world and can understand abstract concepts, such as fairness, justice and peace.

- *Deductive logic*: they understand that it is possible to create rules that help them to test things out, to have a hypothesis and to solve problems.

- *Combinational logic*: they can think in a rational, scientific manner and solve complex problems, for example, algebraic formulas.

Seriation

Montessori cylinder blocks
Each rectangular block has several wooden cylinders that fit into holes ordered from smallest to largest in the block. Children practise their seriating skills by finding the right cylinder for each hole.

Bruner's theory of infant skill development

Bruner proposed that the usual course of intellectual development moves through three stages, as seen in the flow chart below. Unlike Piaget, Bruner did not state that these stages were necessarily age-dependent or inflexible. Bruner's theory has the following features.

Enactive **Iconic** **Symbolic**

Enactive stage

Knowledge is stored primarily in the form of motor responses. This applies to adults as well. Many adults can perform a variety of motor tasks (typing, sewing on a button, operating a lawn mower) that they would find difficult to describe in iconic (picture) or symbolic (word) form. Children need to have real, first-hand, direct experiences; this helps their thought processes to develop.

Iconic stage

Knowledge is stored primarily in the form of visual images. This may explain why, when we are learning a new subject, it is often helpful to have diagrams or illustrations to accompany verbal information. Children need to be reminded of their prior experiences; books and interest tables with objects laid out on them are useful aids to this recall of prior experiences.

Symbolic stage

Knowledge is stored primarily as words, mathematical symbols or in other symbol systems. According to Bruner's classification, these differ from icons in that symbols are arbitrary. For example, the word *beauty* is an arbitrary designation for the idea of beauty in that the word itself is no more inherently beautiful than any other word. Codes are important: languages, music, mathematics, drawing, painting, dance and play are all useful codes which Bruner calls symbolic thinking.

Scaffolding

Adults can help develop children's thinking by being like a piece of scaffolding on a building. At first, the building has a great deal of scaffolding (i.e. adult support of the child's learning) but gradually, as the children extend their competence and control of the situation, the scaffolding is progressively removed until it is no longer needed.

▶ This child has just started learning to walk. The adult is scaffolding the child's attempts to walk by varying the amount of support and encouragement she offers, depending on the child's progress and interest at the time

Scaffolding has particular features:

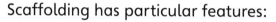

◉ *Recruitment*: the adult's first task is to engage the interest of the child and to encourage them to tackle the requirements of the task.

◉ *Reduction of degrees of freedom*: the adult has to simplify the task by reducing the number of actions required to reach a solution. The child needs to be able to see whether or not they achieved a fit with the task requirements.

◉ *Direction maintenance*: the adult needs to maintain the child's motivation. At first, the child will be looking to the adult for encouragement; eventually, problem-solving should become interesting in its own right.

◉ *Marking critical features*: the adult highlights features of the task that are relevant; this provides information about any inconsistencies between what the child has constructed and what they would perceive as a correct construction.

◉ *Demonstration*: modelling solutions to the task involves completion of a task or explanation of a solution already partly constructed by the child. The aim is that the child will imitate this in an improved form.

Parents routinely act as teachers in the ways outlined above, through rituals and games that are a part of normal adult–child interactions.

Scaffolding

- When a child is trying to describe a new experience, the adult may guide them in the appropriate use of language.
- During a book-reading session with the child, the adult will demonstrate the process by:
  - engaging the child's attention, for example, by saying 'look'
  - simplifying the task by focusing on one question, for example, 'What's that?'
  - maintaining motivation by encouraging any responses
  - giving information about objects in the book, for example, 'It's an X'.

▲ This child is attempting to solve a jigsaw puzzle.

▲ An adult then sits with him and shows some basic strategies, such as finding all the corner and edge pieces.

▲ The adult provides a couple of pieces for the child to put together himself and offers encouragement when he does so. As the child becomes more competent, the adult allows the child to work more independently.

Vygotsky's theory of child development

Lev Vygotsky was born in Russia in the same year as Piaget. His study of cognitive development was greatly influenced by the rise of Marxism in the 1920s. Whereas Piaget was an only child and apparently solitary by nature, Vygotsky was one of eight children, growing up in a culture that valued the importance of the social group. He believed that 'What a child can do in co-operation today he can do alone tomorrow'. The main features of Vygotsky's theory are:

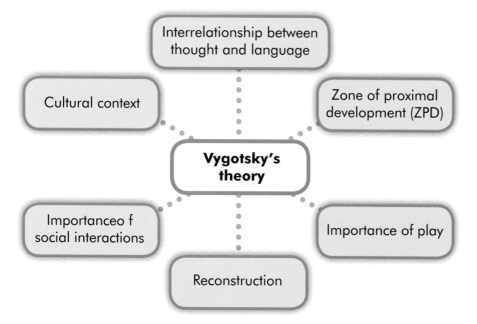

The interrelationship between thought and language

Concepts, language and memory are mental functions that come from the culture and begin with the interaction between the child and another person. Vygotsky maintained that thought is internalised language.

When small children are playing, they often keep up a running commentary on what is happening 'And now the train's going round the tower, and it's banging into the tower, and – oh no – the tower's toppling down …'. Vygotsky calls this an external monologue. As time goes on, the external monologue is internalised as thought.

The zone of proximal development (ZPD)

The ZPD (*proximal* meaning 'next') is defined as the difference between problem solving that the child is capable of performing independently, and problem solving that he or she is capable of performing with guidance or collaboration. This defines the area in which maturation and development is currently taking place and suggests the appropriate target for instruction. Each child has a zone of proximal development that is achievable only with the help and encouragement of another person; this could be guidance from an adult or collaboration with more competent peers. This expert intervention can only enable learning if it is far enough ahead of the child's present level to be a challenge, but not so far ahead that it is beyond comprehension.

The importance of play

Vygotsky believed that play provided foundations for children's developing skills that are essential to social, personal and professional activities. Children benefit from play as it allows them to do things beyond what they can do in real life – such as pretend to drive a car. Play is another way through which children can reach their zone of proximal development.

Reconstruction

Children experience the same situations over and over again as they grow, but each time they can deal with them at a higher level and reconstruct them.

The importance of social interactions

Knowledge is not individually constructed, but is co-constructed between two people. Remember, problem solving, planning and abstract thinking have a social origin. What starts as a social function becomes internalised, so that it occurs within the child.

The cultural context

Children use tools that develop from their own culture, such as speech and writing, to help them to function effectively in society. The history of both the culture and the child's experiences are important for understanding cognitive development.

Freud's theory of personality

Freud believed that the structure of personality involves three parts:

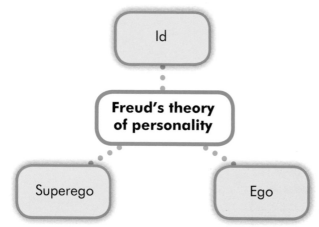

- The **id** contains the drives that people have. The id wants its wishes immediately and directly fulfilled and works on the pleasure principle, which suggests that all processes operate to achieve the maximum amount of pleasure – and to avoid pain. The id is almost completely unconscious. In the newborn infant, all mental processes are id processes.

- The **ego** is the mediator between the id and the superego. As the child grows older, reality intervenes and the ego develops. The ego tries to reconcile the wishes of the id and the moral attitudes of the superego. The ego is governed by the reality principle, which suggests that the person gets as much satisfaction from the world as possible. The ego is rational and logical and allows the child to learn that negotiating, asking and explaining are more effective ways of satisfying demands than through the id's 'I want'.

● The **superego** contains all of the moral lessons the person has learned in their life. It incorporates ideas of duty, obligation and conscience. At around 4 to 6 years old, the child comes into contact with authority and the superego emerges.

Freud's psychosexual stages – a summary

Freud believed that we develop through stages based upon a particular erogenous zone – or pleasure zone. During each stage, an unsuccessful completion means that a child becomes fixated on that particular erogenous zone and either over or under-indulges once he or she becomes an adult. The stages are:

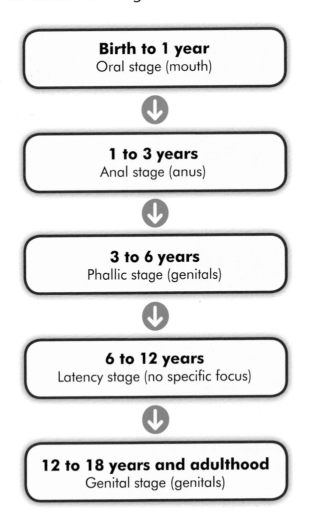

Birth to 1 year
Oral stage (mouth)

↓

1 to 3 years
Anal stage (anus)

↓

3 to 6 years
Phallic stage (genitals)

↓

6 to 12 years
Latency stage (no specific focus)

↓

12 to 18 years and adulthood
Genital stage (genitals)

Birth to I year – oral stage (mouth)

Babies gain satisfaction from putting things into their mouth and sucking. Thumb sucking is defined as fantasy gratification as no milk or food is delivered via the thumb. The earliest attachment is usually to the mother as providing oral gratification. Babies who have not received the optimum amount of oral stimulation – perhaps being weaned too early or too late – become fixated.

Adult behaviour if fixated at this stage: smoking, nail biting, over-eating and passivity.

I to 3 years – anal stage (anus)

Children have their first encounter with rules and regulations, as they have to learn to be toilet trained. The child derives pleasure from having control over the retention and expulsion of faeces. Strict potty training is thought to lead to fixation at this stage.

Adult behaviour if fixated at this stage: obsession with cleanliness, perfection and control (anal retentive personality). On the opposite end of the spectrum, they may become messy and disorganised (anal expulsive personality).

3 to 6 years – phallic stage (genitals)

Boys develop unconscious sexual desires for their mother. Because of this, a boy becomes a rival to his father and sees him as competition for the mother's affection. Boys also develop a fear that their father will punish them for these feelings, such as by castrating them. This group of feelings is known as the Oedipus complex (after the Greek mythology figure who accidentally killed his father and married his mother). Girls go through a similar process, called the Electra complex, which results in identification with the mother. Absence of the appropriate parent at this stage could lead to the child becoming fixated.

Adult behaviour if fixated at this stage: vanity and recklessness and their opposites, modesty and cautiousness.

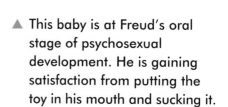

▲ This baby is at Freud's oral stage of psychosexual development. He is gaining satisfaction from putting the toy in his mouth and sucking it.

6 to 12 years – latency stage

Sexual urges remain repressed and children interact and play mostly with same-sex peers. Children often develop 'crushes' on same-sex adults.

Fixation does not usually occur at this stage.

12 to 18 years and adulthood – genital stage (genitals)

At around puberty, children begin to develop an interest in relationships with the opposite sex and during this stage reach mature sexual intimacy.

This stage does not cause any fixation: According to Freud, if people experience difficulties at this stage, and many people do, the damage was done in earlier oral, anal, and phallic stages. For example, attraction to the opposite sex can be a source of anxiety at this stage if the person has not successfully resolved the Oedipal (or Electra) conflict at the phallic stage.

Erikson's theory of psychosocial development

Erikson was an American psychoanalyst who was trained by Anna Freud in child psychoanalysis. Erikson took Sigmund Freud's work as the foundation on which he based his own personality theory. Erikson concentrated on the superego and on the influence of society on a child's development. He showed how, when we meet a personal crisis or have to deal with a crisis in the world (for example, living through a war), we are naturally equipped to face the difficulties and to deal with them.

Erikson's theory has eight distinct stages, each with two possible outcomes. Successful completion of each stage results in a healthy personality and successful interactions with others. Failure to complete a stage successfully can result in a reduced ability to complete further stages and therefore a more unhealthy personality and sense of self. These stages, however, can be resolved successfully at a later time. The stages are:

Trust versus mistrust (birth to 1 year)

Children begin to learn the ability to trust others based upon the consistency of their caregivers. If trust develops successfully, the child gains confidence and security in the world around them and is able to feel secure even when threatened. Unsuccessful completion of this stage can result in an inability to trust and therefore a sense of fear about the inconsistent world. It may result in anxiety, heightened insecurities and an excessive feeling of mistrust in the world around them.

Autonomy versus shame and doubt (1 to 3 years)

Children begin to assert their independence, by walking away from their mother, choosing which toy to play with and making choices about what they like to wear, to eat etc. If children in this stage are encouraged and supported in their increased independence, they become more confident and secure in their own ability to survive in the world. If children are criticised, overly controlled or not given the opportunity to assert themselves, they begin to feel inadequate in their ability to survive and may then lack self-esteem and feel a sense of shame or doubt in their own abilities.

Initiative versus guilt (3 to 6 years)

Children assert themselves more frequently. They begin to plan activities, make up games and initiate activities with others. If given this opportunity, children develop a sense of initiative and feel secure in their ability to lead others and make decisions. However, if this tendency is stifled, either through criticism or control, children develop a sense of guilt. They may feel like a nuisance to others and will therefore remain followers, lacking in self-initiative.

Birth to 1 year
Trust versus mistrust

1 to 3 years
Autonomy versus shame and doubt

3 to 6 years
Initiative versus guilt

6 years to puberty
Industry versus inferiority

Adolescence (12 to 18 years)
Identity versus role confusion

Young adulthood (20s)
Intimacy versus isolation

Mature adulthood (late 20s to 50s)
Generativity versus stagnation

Old age (50s and beyond)
Ego integrity versus despair

Industry versus inferiority (6 to puberty)

Children begin to develop a sense of pride in their accomplishments. They initiate projects, see them through to completion and feel good about what they have achieved. During this time, teachers play an increased role in the child's development. If children are encouraged and reinforced for their initiative, they begin to feel industrious and feel confident in their ability to achieve goals. If this initiative is not encouraged, the child begins to feel inferior, doubting their own abilities and therefore may not reach their potential.

Identity versus role confusion (adolescence: 12 to 18 years)

Children and young people are becoming more independent and begin to look at the future in terms of career, relationships, families etc. During this period, they explore possibilities and begin to form their own identity based upon the outcome of their explorations. This sense of who they are can be stalled, which results in a sense of confusion ('I don't know what I want to be when I grow up') about themselves and their role in the world.

▲ These children have co-operated and developed their own play activity. They are at Erikson's third stage of psychosocial development: initiative versus guilt.

Intimacy versus isolation (young adulthood: 20s)

People explore relationships leading towards longer-term commitments with someone other than a family member. Successful completion can lead to comfortable relationships and a sense of commitment, security and care within a relationship. Avoiding intimacy and fearing commitment and relationships can lead to isolation, loneliness and sometimes depression.

Generativity versus stagnation (mature adulthood: late 20s to 50s)

People establish careers, settle down within a relationship, begin their own families and develop a sense of community. By failing to achieve these objectives, they become stagnant and feel unproductive.

Ego integrity versus despair (old age: 50s and beyond)

People contemplate their accomplishments and are able to develop integrity if they see themselves as leading a successful life. If they see their lives as unproductive, feel guilt about the past or feel that they did not accomplish their life goals, they become dissatisfied with life and develop despair, often leading to depression and hopelessness.

Bowlby's theory of maternal deprivation and attachment

Bowlby stated that a child's personality development is achieved through a close continuous relationship with their mother. These are the main principles of Bowlby's theory:

- the first five years of life are the most important in a person's development

- a child's relationship with its parents (in particular with the mother) has an enormous effect on the child's overall development

- separation from a parent, particularly from the mother, is a major cause of psychological trauma in childhood

- such separation and consequent psychological trauma has long-lasting effects on the overall development of the child

- the attachment is **monotropic** (this means that it is established between the infant and one other person)

- there is a critical period for attachment formation. Bowlby thought that the period between 6 months and 3 years was critical for attachment formation. The child *must* form an attachment by about 6 months after which, until around 3 years, they have a strong need to be continuously with or close to their main carer (usually the mother). Any obstacle to the forming of an attachment, or any subsequent disruption of the relationship, constitutes maternal deprivation.

- the secure attachment and continuous relationship a child needs is far more likely to be provided within their natural family than anywhere else.

▲ This child has a secure attachment to her mother. Bowlby believed that the period between 6 months and 3 years was critical for attachment formation.

There has been confusion over the terms bonding and attachment. Bonding has at times been portrayed as an almost mystical experience for mothers following the birth of their child. While some mothers do have this experience, many do not. Attachment is a two-way process which develops over time. Bowlby did not say that the most important attachment figure *must* be the natural mother. He did stress, however, that babies need one central person who is the mother figure. Both the primary caregiver and the infant are active participants in this process. The key factor for the caregiver is sensitive responsiveness – the ability to attune to the child and respond to their signals. The child's responsiveness is also an important contributor to the process. Attachment problems are more likely to arise with temperamentally 'difficult' babies.

Glossary

adolescence The period of psychological and social transition between childhood and adulthood, basically covering the teenage years.

animism The belief that all objects possess consciousness.

anterior fontanelle A diamond-shaped soft area at the front of the head in a young baby, just above the brow. It is a temporary gap between the bones of the head, and is covered by a tough membrane – often you can see the baby's pulse beating beneath the skin. The fontanelle closes between 12 and 18 months of age, when the bones fuse together.

articulation A person's actual pronunciation of words.

attachment An enduring emotional bond that an infant forms with a specific person. Often the first attachment is to the mother, some time between the ages of 6 and 9 months.

attention deficit disorder (ADD) A behavioural disorder characterised by an inability to concentrate on tasks. In attention deficit hyperactivity disorder (ADHD), inability to concentrate is accompanied or replaced by hyperactive and impulsive behaviour.

autism (autistic spectrum disorder) Ar are developmental disorder which impairs a child's understanding of, and their ability to relate to, the environment.

bonding A term used to denote the feelings of love and responsibility that parents have for their babies.

British Sign Language (BSL) One of the languages used by those with a hearing impairment. To conduct a conversation, language users make gestures involving movements of their hands, arms, eyes, face and body.

casting Repeatedly throwing objects to the floor, in play or rejection.

cataract The loss of transparency of the crystalline lens of the eye.

central nervous system (CNS) Theb rain and the spinal cord, which are the main control centres of the body.

cerebral palsy A general term for disorders of movement and posture resulting from damage to the child's developing brain.

class inclusion The understanding – more advanced than simple classification – that some classes or sets of objects are also sub-sets of a larger class. For example, there is a class of objects called cats. There is also a class called animals. But all cats are also animals, so the class of animals includes that of cats.

cleft palate A hole or split in the palate (the roof of the mouth).

coeliac disease A condition in which the lining of the small intestine is damaged by gluten, a protein found in wheat and certain other cereals.

cognitive (intellectual) Related to the ideas and thinking of the child. Cognition emphasises that children are aware, active learners, and that understanding is an important part of intellectual life.

comfort object (transitional object) An object, such as a blanket, a piece of cloth or a teddy, to which a child becomes especially attached.

communication Facial expression, body language, gestures, and verbal or sign language; talking about feelings, ideas and relationships using signs or words. (Language involves both reception – understanding – and expression.)

concept An overall idea formed in the mind, which is based on and links past, present and future ideas that share some attributes. Thus a child may sit on a variety of actual chairs, but the concept of 'a chair' is an idea that develops in the child's mind.

conservation The concept that objects remain the same in basic ways, such as their weight or number, even when there are external changes in their shape or arrangement.

co-operative play Play in which children take account of other children's actions or roles within their play together – for instance, one might be the baby, the other the nurse, and the nurse might give medical treatment to the baby.

cradle test See Otoacoustic Emissions Testing.

creative play See imaginative play.

creativity The ability to make something from an idea one has imagined, for example a dance, a model, a poem or a mathematical equation; the process of creating something.

Down's syndrome A genetic anomaly, which results in children having learning difficulties and characteristic physical features. Also known as Down Syndrome.

dynamic tripod grasp Using the thumb and two fingers in a grip closely resembling the adult grip of a pencil or pen. *Compare* primitive tripod grasp.

dyslexia A specific reading disability, characterised by difficulty in coping with written symbols.

dyspraxia An immaturity of the brain such that some messages are not transmitted to the body. Children with dyspraxia often show behavioural difficulties and may be hyperactive.

echolalia The tendency of a child to echo the last words spoken by an adult.

egocentric Self-centred, or viewing things from one's own standpoint.

ejaculation The process of ejecting semen from the penis; it is usually accompanied by orgasm as a result of sexual stimulation. It may also occur spontaneously during sleep (called a nocturnal emission or wet dream).

empathy Awareness of another person's emotional state, and the ability to share the experience with that person.

epididymis A storage chamber in the male's body, which is attached to each testicle. This is where sperm cells are nourished and mature.

erection When the penis becomes stiff and hard due to increased blood flow. Erections may happen in response to physical or emotional stimulation, or sometimes an erection happens for no reason at all.

evaluate To find out or judge the value of something.

expression Communication of what one thinks, feels or means, by word, facial expression, gesture or sign language.

expressive speech The words a person produces.

extension Stretching out.

fallopian tubes Narrow tubes that are connected to the uterus. The fringes of the fallopian tube catch the egg cell when it is released from the ovary, and the egg cell then slowly travels from the ovary, down the fallopian tube, to the uterus.

fantasy play Play in which children role-play situations they do not fully know about, but which might happen to them one day, such as going to hospital or travelling to the moon in a space rocket.

fine manipulative skills Skills involving precise use of the hands and fingers in pointing, drawing, using a knife and fork, using chopsticks, writing and doing up shoelaces.

fine motor skills Skills including gross manipulative skills, which involve single limb movements, and fine manipulative skills, which involve precise movements of the hands and fingers.

flexion Bending.

gay A term used to describe men and women who are sexually attracted to people of their own sex.

gender identity The psychological sense a person has of being male or female.

genitals The external sex organs.

gesture Any movement intended to convey meaning.

giftedness Having unusually great ability over a wide range of skills.

grooming Deliberately befriending and establishing an emotional connection with a child to lower the child's inhibitions in order to move on to the next stage: sexual activity or exploitation.

gross manipulative skills Skills involving single limb movements, usually of the arm, for example in throwing, catching and sweeping arm movements.

gross motor skills Skills involving the use of the large muscles in the body; they include walking, running and climbing.

growth (centile) chart A graph or chart used to plot the growth measurements (height and weight) of babies and children.

growth spurt A rapid growth of bone and muscle occurring at various ages from infancy to puberty.

heterosexism The belief and practice that heterosexuality is the only natural form of sexuality, and the belief that being heterosexual is better than being homosexual.

heterosexual Feeling sexually attracted to people of the opposite sex.

holistic Tending to see something in the round, for example seeing a child as a whole person, emotionally, intellectually, socially, physically, morally, culturally and spiritually.

holophrase The expression of a whole idea in a single word: thus 'car' may mean 'Give me the car' or 'Look at the car'.

homophobia Negative or fearful attitudes to homosexuality.

homosexual Feeling sexually attracted to people of the same sex.

hormones Chemical messengers created by glands that control specific things that happen in the body.

hypothalamus An area of the brain responsible for controlling functions such as regulating fluid balance, body temperature, sleep, food intake and the development of the body during puberty.

ICT Informationc ommunication technology: the computing and communications facilities and features that variously support teaching, learning and a range of activities in education. The most obvious example of this is computers, but it can also mean televisions, videos, DVDs, CDs, cassette recorders, telephones, musical keyboards and fax machines.

imagination The ability to form new ideas, which, though they may emerge from first-hand experiences of life, go beyond what one has experienced.

imaginative play (creative play) Play in which children draw on their own real-life experiences and rearrange them – for instance, they might make a pretend swimming pool from wooden blocks and then play out a rescue scene in which a child is saved from drowning in the pool by a lifeguard.

inclusive care and education Th e integration of disabled children into mainstream settings such as nursery schools, day nurseries, schools and family centres.

intellectual *See* cognitive.

labile Having rapidly fluctuating moods, such as cheerful one moment and angry the next.

language A structured system of communication that conveys meaning.

lesbian Refers to women who are sexually attracted to other women. The word gay can also be used.

LGBT An abbreviation for lesbian, gay, bisexual and transgender people.

literacy The ability to read and write: writing involves putting spoken language into a written code; reading involves decoding the written code into language.

Makaton A method of sign language that uses a combination of manual signs, graphic symbols and speech (the Makaton vocabulary) to support spoken English.

menarche The first menstrual period.

meningitis Inflammation of the meninges membranes that enclose the brain and spinal cord.

menstruation The process by which the lining of the uterus is shed periodically as menstrual flow. It usually happens about once a month except during pregnancy.

metacognition A loosely used term describing an individual's knowledge of their own thinking processes. It means that you know both what you know and how you manage to remember and learn.

motor development Growth and change in the ability to carry out physical activities, such as walking, running or riding a bicycle.

neuroscience Studies of the central nervous system, (the brain and spinal cord), which provide evidence to help early years specialists working with young children.

nocturnal emission An ejaculation of semen that happens while a boy is sleeping. It is sometimes called a wet dream, and is the natural way of making room for new sperm cells that are made.

norm An average or typical state or ability, used with others as a framework for assessing development. Norms are the result of observations by many professionals in the field of child development.

normative Relating to norms or averages.

object permanence The recognition that an object continues to exist even when temporarily out of sight.

observation The process of watching accurately and taking notice.

oestrogen The main female sex hormone produced by the ovaries.

orgasm A pleasurable physical or emotional response to sexual stimulation; it is also known as a sexual climax.

Otoacoustic Emissions Testing (OAE or cradle test) A hearing test. It is often called the cradle test because it is performed on newborn babies.

ovaries Two small organs inside a female's body where egg cells are produced and stored. Each ovary is about the size of a walnut, and there is one on each side of the uterus. The ovaries also produce the hormones oestrogen and progesterone.

ovulation The release of an egg cell by an ovary. This process usually occurs at the midpoint of the menstrual cycle.

ovum Another name for the female egg cell. It is smaller than a grain of salt.

paediatrician A qualified doctor who specialises in treating children.

palmar grasp Using the whole hand to grasp an object.

parallel play Play in which one child plays alongside another child, but without interacting with the other child.

penis The male reproductive organ involved in sexual intercourse and elimination of urine.

perception The process by which events and information in the environment are transformed into an experience of objects, sounds, events and the like.

period The days when menstruation is taking place.

personality The total combination of mental and behavioural characteristics that make each individual recognisably unique. Personality is affected by children's experiences of life and other people, as well as by the child's natural temperament.

pincer grasp Using the thumb and fingers to grasp an object.

Picture Exchange Communication System (PECS) A communication system using picture symbols – rather than words or signing – within a social context.

pituitary gland A small gland at the base of the brain, which is responsible for controlling the hormones that affect growth, metabolism and maturation.

Portage A planned approach to home-based pre-school education for children with developmental delay, disabilities or other special educational needs.

posterior fontanelle A small triangular-shaped soft area near the crown of the head. It is a temporary gap between the bones of the head, and is much smaller and less noticeable than the anterior fontanelle. It usually closes by 6 to 8 weeks of age.

pretend play Play in which an action or object is given a symbolic meaning other than that from real life, such as when a clothes peg is used to represent a door key, or a large box to represent a boat.

primary sexual characteristics The penis and testes in males and the vagina and ovaries in females. Compare secondary sexual characteristics.

primitive reflexes Automatic reactions to particular changes in surroundings – present in the newborn baby, and thought to be vital for the infant's survival. Reflexes give an indication of the baby's general condition and the normal functioning of the central nervous system. See also reflex.

primitive tripod grasp Grasping objects by use of the thumb and two fingers. Compare dynamic tripod grasp.

progesterone A female hormone.

prone Lying on one's face, or front downward. Compare supine.

proprioception The sense that tells infants where the mobile parts of their body (such as their legs) are in relation to the rest of them.

prostate gland A male gland at the base of the bladder. It produces a thin, milky fluid that makes up the largest part of the semen.

puberty The stage of growth in which a child's body turns into the body of an adult. The child or young person experiences physical, hormonal and sexual changes, and becomes capable of reproduction. It is associated with rapid growth and the appearance of secondary sexual characteristics.

reception (of language) Listening to or watching and understanding language.

receptive speech The words a person understands.

reflex An automatic response to a stimulus. See also primitive reflexes.

role-play Play in which 'pretend' symbols are used together with an activity – for example, a child pretends that a box is a car and then 'drives' to the shops.

scaffolding A term used by, among others, Jerome Bruner, for describing the support given to a child in order for them to construct and extend skills to higher levels of competence, during which the scaffolding is slowly removed.

schema Children's patterns of learning; linked actions and behaviours that the child can generalise and use in a variety of different situations, e.g. up, down, in, out etc.

scrotum The outside sac of loose skin under the penis that holds the testicles.

secondary sexual characteristics Traits that distinguish the two sexes of a species, but which are not directly part of the reproductive system, e.g. enlarged breasts in females and pubic hair in both sexes.

self-concept How a child sees himself or herself; how the child believes others see him or her.

self-esteem The way a child feels about herself or himself: good feelings lead to high self-esteem, bad feelings lead to low self-esteem.

semen A milky white fluid made by the seminal vesicles and prostate gland. This fluid mixes with the sperm cells during an ejaculation. A teaspoonful or more of semen comes out of the penis during an ejaculation.

seminal vesicle One of two glands located behind the male bladder, which secrete a fluid that forms part of semen.

sensation Being aware of having an experience, through seeing, smelling, hearing, touching, tasting or moving (kinaesthesia).

seriation The ability to arrange things in a logical order, such as arranging a set of sticks according to increasing or decreasing length.

sexual intercourse The erect penis of the male entering the vagina of the female.

sexual orientation An enduring emotional, romantic and sexual attraction to a particular sex.

Signalong A method of signing (using gestures and symbols) used with children who have communication difficulties.

small-world play Play that involves the use of miniature objects, such as doll's houses, toy farms and zoos, dinosaur models and play-people.

smooth pursuit *See* tracking.

socialisation The process by which children learn the culture or way of life of the society into which they have been born.

solitary play (solo play) Play in which a child plays alone, exploring and experimenting with objects.

spectator play Play in which children watch what others do, but do not join in.

sperm The microscopic cells produced by a male that contains the genes from the father. A sperm cell from the father must join with an egg cell from the mother for a baby to be created.

spina bifida A condition in which one or more of the vertebrae in the backbone fail to form, as a result of which the spinal cord may be damaged and/or exposed. Spina bifida may be mild; in its severest form, however, it can cause widespread paralysis and a wide range of physical disabilities.

supine Lying on one's back, or face upwards. *Compare* prone.

symbolism Making one thing stand for another.

syntax The study of the rules that govern the ways in which words combine to form phrases, clauses, and sentences. Syntax is one of the major components of grammar.

talipes A condition in which the foot is not in the correct alignment with the leg; it is sometimes called 'club foot'.

telegraphic speech (telegraphese)Th e abbreviation of a sentence such that only the crucial words are spoken, as in a telegram – for instance, 'Where daddy going?' or 'Shut door'.

temperament The style of behaviour that comes naturally, as, for example, a general tendency to be relaxed or excitable.

testes The medical name for testicles.(The singular is testis.)

testicles The main male reproductive glands in which sperm are produced. The testicles also produce the main male hormone, testosterone.

testosterone A male sex hormone, which causes a boy's body to develop into a man's. Testosterone is responsible for promoting more muscle mass, a deeper voice and facial hair.

Theory of Mind The ability to understand that other people have different beliefs and desires to own.

tracking (smooth pursuit) The smooth movements made by the eyes in following the track of a moving object.

transitional object *See* comfort object.

transsexual Having a body with one set of sexual characteristics but feeling emotionally that you are the opposite sex.

uterus Another name for the womb.

ventral suspension Supporting a baby in a prone position with a hand under the abdomen.

weaning The introduction of solid food to a baby's diet, at the age of 4–6 months.

References and further reading

Bee, H. (1992) *The Developing Child*, New York: HarperCollins

Bruce, T. (1996) *Helping Young Children to Play*, London: Hodder Arnold

Bruce, T., Meggitt, C. and Grenier, J. (2010) *Child Care and Education (5th edition)*, London: Hodder Education

Cole, M. and Cole, S.R. (1993) *The Development of Children*, New York: Scientific American

Einon, D. (1986) *Creative Play*, London: Penguin Books

Gopnik, A., Meltzoff, A. and Kuhl, P. (2001) *How Babies Think: The Science of Childhood*, London: Pheonix

Karmiloff-Smith, A. (1994) *Baby It's You*, London: Ebury Press

Landsdowne, R. and Walker, M. (1997) *Your Child's Development from Birth to Adolescence*, London: Frances Lincoln

Meggitt, C. (2001) *Baby and Child Health (Professional Development)*, Oxford: Heinemann

Meggitt, C. (2012) *Understand Child Development*, T each Yourself: London: Hodder

Nyssen, C. (2003) *Baby Massage for the VTCT Certificate*, Oxford: Heinemann

Sheridan, M.D., Sharma, A. and Frost, M. (1997) *From Birth to Five Years: Children's Developmental Progress*, London: Routledge

Thomson, H. and Meggitt, C. (1997) *Human Growth and Development for Health and Social Care*, London: Hodder Education

Usefulw ebsites

Action for Sick Children

www.actionforsickchildren.org

Advisory Centre for Education (ACE)

www.ace-ed.org.uk

ChildGro wthF oundation

www.childgrowthfoundation.org

Contact a Family

Contact a Family helps families who care for children with any disability or special need.

www.cafamily.org.uk

Council for Disabled Children

www.ncb.org.uk

Cystic Fibrosis Trust

www.cftrust.org.uk

Down's Syndrome Association

www.downs-syndrome.org.uk

DyslexiaAc tion

www.dyslexiaaction.org.uk

EarlyS upport

Early Support is a national programme to help families with a disabled child to identify services that can help them, and to ensure that the services work together in a co-ordinated way.

www.direct.gov.uk/en/CaringForSomeone/
CaringForADisabledChild/DG_I80I65

Home-StartUK

Home-Start schemes offer friendship, support and practical advice to families in difficulties with children under 5 in their homes.

www.home-start.org.uk

ICAN

I CAN helps children with a communication disability.

www.ican.org.uk

KIDS

KIDS helps disabled children to get the most out of life.

www.kids.org.uk

MENCAP

Royal Society for Mentally Handicapped Children and Adults

www.mencap.org.uk

Muscular Dystrophy Group of Great Britain and Northern Ireland

www.muscular-dystrophy.org

National Asthma Campaign, Asthma UK

www.asthma.org.uk

National Autistic Society

The NAS aims to champion the rights and interests of all people with autism, and to provide individuals with autism and their families with help, support and services.

www.autism.org.uk

National Deaf Children's Society (NDCS)

www.ndcs.org.uk

National Eczema Society (NES)

www.eczema.org

Pre-School Learning Alliance

www.pre-school.org.uk

REACH

The Association for Children with Upper Limb Deficiency

www.reach.org.uk

Royal Institute for the Blind (RNIB)

www.rnib.org.uk

SCOPE

Scope is a charity that supports disabled people and their families, specialising in people who have cerebral palsy.

www.scope.org.uk

SEBDA

SEBDA serves the interests of children and young people experiencing difficulties in their social, emotional and behavioural development.

www.sebda.org

SENSE

National Deaf-Blind and Rubella Association

www.sense.org.uk

SHINE

Previously the Association for Spina Bifida and Hydrocephalus(ASBAH).

www.shinecharity.org.uk